teach®
yourself

**PC networking for
your small business**

PC networking for
your small business

anthony price

For UK order enquiries: please contact Bookpoint Ltd, 130 Milton Park, Abingdon, Oxon OX14 4SB. Telephone: +44 (0)1235 827720. Fax: +44 (0)1235 400454. Lines are open 09.00–17.00, Monday to Saturday, with a 24-hour message answering service. Details about our titles and how to order are available at www.teachyourself.co.uk.

For USA order enquiries: please contact McGraw-Hill Customer Services, PO Box 545, Blacklick, OH 43004-0545, USA. Telephone: 1-800-722-4726. Fax: 1-614-755-5645.

For Canada order enquiries: please contact McGraw-Hill Ryerson Ltd, 300 Water St, Whitby, Ontario L1N 9B6, Canada. Telephone: 905 430 5000. Fax: 905 430 5020.

Long renowned as the authoritative source for self-guided learning – with more than 50 million copies sold worldwide – the **teach yourself** series includes over 500 titles in the fields of languages, crafts, hobbies, business, computing and education.

British Library Cataloguing in Publication Data: a catalogue record for this title is available from The British Library.

Library of Congress Catalog Card Number: on file.

First published in UK 2007 by Hodder Education, 338 Euston Road, London NW1 3BH.

First published in US 2007 by The McGraw-Hill Companies Inc.

The **teach yourself** name is a registered trademark of Hodder Headline.

Computer hardware and software brand names mentioned in this book are protected by their respective trademarks and are acknowledged.

The publisher has used its best endeavours to ensure that the URLs for external websites referred to in this book are correct and active at the time of going to press. However, the publisher has no responsibility for the websites and can give no guarantee that a site will remain live or that the content is or will remain appropriate.

Typeset by MacDesign, Southampton

Printed in Great Britain for Hodder Education, a division of Hodder Headline, 338 Euston Road, London NW1 3BH, by Cox & Wyman Ltd, Reading, Berkshire.

Hodder Headline's policy is to use papers that are natural, renewable and recyclable products and made from wood grown in sustainable forests. The logging and manufacturing processes are expected to conform to the environmental regulations of the country of origin.

Impression number   10 9 8 7 6 5 4 3 2 1

Year   2011 2010 2009 2008 2007

contents

preface

The simple business truth about PC networks is that they save you time and money. They also play a key role in managing and protecting one of your most valuable business assets – data. Whether you are linking two PCs to share a broadband connection and a printer, or thinking of a secure client/server network of 20 or so machines, *Teach Yourself PC Networking for your Small Business* will tell you what you need to know. It takes a common sense approach to the practicalities of small scale workplace PC networks – the everyday business of sharing resources and providing services in the small enterprise.

The book is suitable for:

* Sole traders and professional partnerships
* Businesses without full-time IT support staff
* PC technicians who want to acquire some basic networking skills
* Schools and voluntary organizations
* Ambitious home users.

All of the equipment used in the examples in the book is commonplace everyday kit that can be bought from the local PC retailer or one of the online shops. The book assumes that you are using one of the modern versions of the Windows Operating System such as XP or Vista, and that you are familiar with the basics of using a Windows-based PC.

Most of the examples in the text have been tested using XP Professional, though there will be variations and differences between this version of Windows and others such as XP Home and Vista. For the most part, the differences between Windows versions are unimportant – where they are, it is noted in the text.

If you have no experience of PC maintenance you may find a copy of *Teach Yourself Home PC Maintenance and Networking* a useful companion to this book.

Teach Yourself PC Networking for your Small Business is grouped under four themes: networking basics (Chapters 1–6), maintaining a network (Chapters 7–11), and client/server systems (Chapters 12–14), staff training and troubleshooting (Chapters 15 and 16).

Networking basics

There are many books and training courses on PC networks and the theoretical aspects can be hair-raising in their complexity. The good news is that 90 odd per cent of this material isn't needed for you to plan, implement, and manage a small business PC network. What you do need, however, is to understand some of the basic principles of a Local Area Network (LAN) using easily available equipment and straightforward techniques.

With this in mind, the first chapter looks at how to get two PCs to 'talk' to one another over a single 'crossover' cable. Later chapters build on this: sharing resources such as printers and Internet connections, expanding your network to include more than two PCs, the practicalities of cabling and the basics of wireless networking and configuring Internet and e-mail services. Planning your network is at the end of this section – once you have grasped the basics you will be in a stronger position to make informed choices about your network infrastructure.

Maintaining a network

Two of the most important differences between the home network and that of even the smallest business are the value of the data and the amount of down-time that is acceptable in the event of an equipment failure. If, as a home user, you lose the family photos and your system is unusable for a couple of days because of a failure it will be annoying (possibly very annoying) but it won't put you out of business.

Fault tolerance and disaster recovery are as necessary for the small enterprise as for the large one. Fortunately, the techniques needed to keep your data safe and minimizing down-time are straightforward. These chapters look at backups and fault tolerant configurations such as RAID arrays on a scale suited to the small enterprise. The ability to install an operating system and applications as a ready-to-go replacement for a failed workstation are examined in this section of the book, as are unattended installing techniques for Windows and the deployment tools necessary for 'cloning' drives.

Client/server systems

Client/server systems are often thought to be the exclusive domain of the larger enterprise, but this need not be the case. There are some disadvantages to a client/server system – not least the fact that someone has to be the overall system administrator/manager. However, the advantages of client/server can be considerable particularly in terms of security and data integrity.

These chapters look at some of the network operating systems (NOS) which meet the needs of the small enterprise and develops one of them – the Linux-based SME 7. This system is free for non-profit organizations, educational establishments and home users. You may need a paid-for software licence for commercial use. This section does not cover everything there is to be known about client/server networks – it deals only with a single server small network suitable for the needs of the small enterprise.

Printing and security topics are discussed in these chapters, though they are not, of course, exclusive to client/server setups.

Staff training and troubleshooting

The final two chapters look at staff training and troubleshooting. Generally speaking, the more you do of the first of these, the less you will have to do of the second. If staff are knowledgeable and confident in their use of the system they will make fewer support requests, or where they do make a support request it will be more concise and useful in tracking down the problem.

Troubleshooting is, of course, inevitable – not every problem is understood or fixed easily (though many are) – so there are tested techniques and diagnostic tools that have been developed by professional support workers over the years. These techniques, tailored to the needs of the small enterprise, make up the final chapter of the book.

About you

You own, manage, or are involved in the running of a small business, charity or other small enterprise. Possibly you are the IT support worker – official or otherwise. You are aware of the advantages of networking the PCs in a small business. Possibly you are planning a network, or maybe just trying to make sense of an existing small network that just grew. Whatever your situation, you are willing and able to have a go, to experiment, and even to get it wrong a few times on the way to getting it right. Whether you choose to do everything in-house or to contract some of the more technical aspects to someone else, *Teach Yourself PC Networking for your Small Business* will enable you to make informed choices in planning, implementing and maintaining a small workplace LAN.

Acknowledgements

Thanks are due to Tracey Williams for reading the original typescript with the eye of an A+ qualified working PC technician, for checking the examples, and for correcting a number of errors. Any errors which remain are, of course, my responsibility.

Anthony Price
anthonyp@elenmar.com
2007

About the author

Teach Yourself PC Networking for your Small Business has been written for the small business user by an experienced teacher and working Field Engineer. The author teaches computer maintenance and networking at an Adult Education College and has published a book aimed at professional PC technicians: *A+ for Students* (Hodder Arnold) and *Teach Yourself Home PC Maintenance and Networking*. He holds a Master of Science degree in Information Technology.

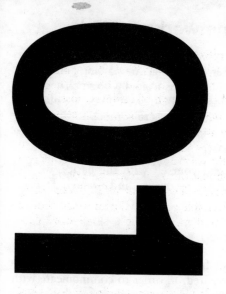

01

getting started

In this chapter you will learn:

- how to fit a network adaptor card
- how to connect 2 PCs with a crossover cable
- how to test your connection
- some basic Local Area Network (LAN) terminology

1.1 Local area networks (LANs)

The smallest possible PC network consists of just two machines that can 'talk' to each other, and this is our starting point. Most of the technicalities and problems associated with small networks can be explored by using just two PCs. Even if you are planning to have a larger network than this, there is much to be said for working through the material presented in this chapter on a couple of machines given over to the task.

When you have familiarized yourself with the basics, we will extend the network to share resources and to include some additional PCs and users.

Network adaptors

The type of network most frequently used today is Ethernet – which may be wireless or wired. In order to communicate with each other, each of the PCs on our two-node network needs to have a working network adaptor, sometimes known as a network interface card (NIC) or even just a network card.

Wireless networking is the main topic of Chapter 4, *Wireless networks* – in this chapter we are concerned only with a cable connection between the two boxes.

Most modern desktop PCs and nearly all laptop/notebook systems have an Ethernet adaptor built in as part of the motherboard. Check if this is the case with your PC:

• Navigate to **Start > Control Panel > Network Connections.**

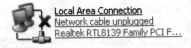

Local Area Connection
Network cable unplugged
Realtek RTL8139 Family PCI F...

Figure 1.01

Figure 1.01 shows a working Ethernet port which does not have a cable connected. If this is the case with both of your machines, then you can skip the next sections which show you how to fit an Ethernet adaptor.

USB LAN adaptor

Nearly all modern PCs have Universal Serial Bus (USB) ports on the back and front of the case. They are rectangular in section and are frequently used for attaching printers, cameras, etc.

Several manufacturers supply USB/RJ45 adaptors which allow you to plug an Ethernet cable into a USB port. These work best with USB2 ports and will give an Ethernet connection of up to 100 Mbps (megabits per second) – this standard is known as *Fast Ethernet* – and is pretty much the accepted standard for modern networks.

To use a USB/RJ45 adaptor, plug it into one of the USB ports (Figure 1.02). Windows will recognize it as a USB device and will prompt you for drivers. Follow the on-screen instructions and put the manufacturer's CD in the CD drive when prompted.

Figure 1.02

USB LAN adaptors are well suited to small ad hoc networks, but if you want something faster – or just neater looking – you will have to install an internal Ethernet card in one of the expansion slots on the motherboard. This may be one of the Peripheral Component Interconnect (PCI) slots or the more modern PCI-E slot. Either way the procedure is essentially similar.

1.2 Installing a PCI LAN adaptor

1   Before you start, read the installation instructions that came with the adaptor – these take priority over any general advice.

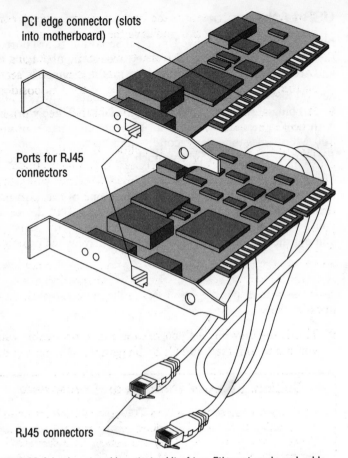

PCI edge connector (slots into motherboard)

Ports for RJ45 connectors

RJ45 connectors

Figure 1.03 A basic networking starter kit of two Ethernet cards and cable.

2 Power down the PC and disconnect it from the mains supply.

3 Remove the side panel or cover from the PC – the exact means of doing this will vary between machines, but you will probably need a Philips #2 screwdriver.

4 Before you touch any component, touch a bare metal part of the PC chassis to eliminate any static in your body. Attach yourself to the chassis with an anti-static wrist strap at this point for extra safety.

5 Locate an unused PCI slot on the motherboard – they are about 8cm long and cream/off-white in colour.

6   Remove the cover plate at the back of the case which corresponds to the empty slot and save the fixing screw.

7   Remove the adaptor card from its anti-static packaging and fit it into the PCI slot. Make sure that it is properly seated, and then use the screw that you saved to fix it in position.

8   Replace the side panel or cover of the PC, reconnect the mains power and turn it on.

Thanks to the Plug and Play capabilities of Windows, the new card will be detected as the PC reboots. If you have chosen one of the more popular network cards, then Windows will provide and install the necessary software drivers and report the card as being ready to use.

In the event of Windows not having the required drivers, you will have to install them from the manufacturer's CD. Windows will usually prompt you to provide drivers, so all you need to do is to follow the on-screen instructions. Alternatively, you can close the wizard, put the driver CD in the drive and click on the installer icon.

9   This is the easy bit. All you need is a crossover cable which you use to join the two PCs by plugging it in at each end.

Cables: straight-through and crossover

The Ethernet cables that are most commonly used are rated as Category 5, 5e or 6 (described more fully in Chapter 3, *Cables and connectors*). They are usually of the straight-through type, that is, each of the eight lines of the cable attach to the same pins on the RJ45 connector at each end. A crossover cable is a variant which is used to connect two PCs without using a hub or a switch, and to achieve this, the transmit and receive lines are crossed over. You can make them yourself, or buy them preformed.

To network your two PCs, make sure that you are using a crossover cable – if you bought it preformed it will be marked as such. Push the RJ45 connector on the cable end into the port on the PC at each end. There is a retaining clip on the connector and you should hear and feel it engaging with the port.

After a few seconds – half a minute, perhaps – the two PCs will see one another, provided that they are members of the same workgroup. By default, Windows PCs are members of the workgroup called WORKGROUP.

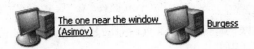

Figure 1.04

Figure 1.04 shows the members of the workgroup, in this case ASIMOV and BURGESS, our two-PC network.

A very simple test for connectivity between any two PCs on your network is to use the PING command.

1 Use the menu command **Start > All Programs > Accessories > Command Prompt**.

2 Click on the **Command Prompt** icon. This launches a command line processor.

3 To see if ASIMOV can be seen from BURGESS, type the command line 'PING ASIMOV', followed by [**Enter**].

```
C:\>PING ASIMOV

Pinging ASIMOV [169.254.187.195] with 32 bytes of data:

Reply from 169.254.187.195: bytes=32 time<1ms TTL=128
Reply from 169.254.187.195: bytes=32 time<1ms TTL=128
Reply from 169.254.187.195: bytes=32 time<1ms TTL=128
Reply from 169.254.187.195: bytes=32 time<1ms TTL=128

Ping statistics for 169.254.187.195:
    Packets: Sent = 4, Received = 4, Lost = 0 <0% loss>,
Approximate round trip times in milli-seconds:
    Minimum = 0ms, Maximum = 0ms, Average = 0ms
```

Figure 1.05

Note: In Figure 1.05, capital letters are used on the command line as an aid to clarity. In practice you can use upper case, lower case, or any combination of the two.

If you have followed the instructions so far, you should have two PCs that can see one another, i.e. you can PING either of them from the other. If you are having problems, there are a few things to check.

- **Physical connections** – double-check that you are using a crossover cable and that it is properly engaged in the ports at each end. Also check the lights on the network card. These vary between cards, but there should be at least one indicator which is lit to show a connection and another which will flicker during data transmission. If there are no lights, you may need to power down the PC and reseat the network card.

- **Firewall** – check that your firewall (Windows or third-party) is allowing connections across your LAN. Providing you are not connected to the Internet, you could simply disable the firewall for long enough to PING your connection in order to test it. Don't forget that when sharing an Internet connection only the PC which is connected to the Internet needs a firewall in place. Chapter 9, *Internet and e-mail* looks at firewalls in more detail.

- **Workgroup membership** – To check or change the workgroup for your PC:

1 Right-click on the **My Computer** icon and select **Properties** from the context menu, then select the **Computer Name** tab. To change the computer, workgroup or domain name, click **Change**. You will be presented with a dialog box like the one in Figure 1.06.

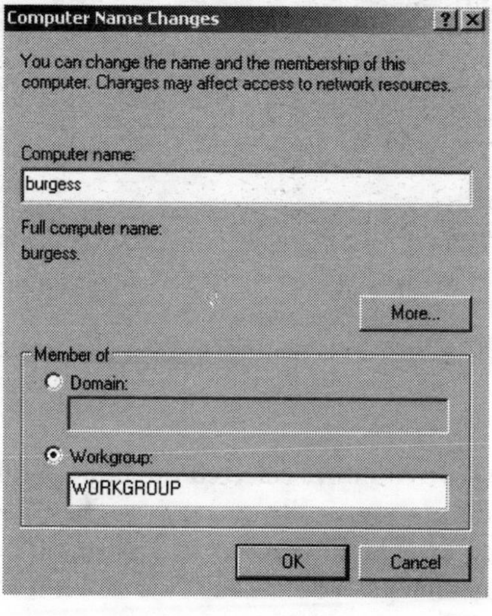

Computer Name Changes

You can change the name and the membership of this computer. Changes may affect access to network resources.

Computer name:
burgess

Full computer name:
burgess.

More...

Member of

Domain:

Workgroup:
WORKGROUP

OK   Cancel

Figure 1.06

2 Enter the required changes and click **OK**. You will be prompted to restart the PC to make the changes work.

3 By default, Windows PCs are set to obtain an IP address automatically. To check this, navigate to **Control Panel > Network Connections**, then right-click on the icon for your network adaptor – choose **Properties** from the context menu and highlight the **Internet Protocol (TCP/IP)** entry in the list, as in Figure 1.07.

Figure 1.07

4 Click **Properties**. This will bring up a dialog box like this.

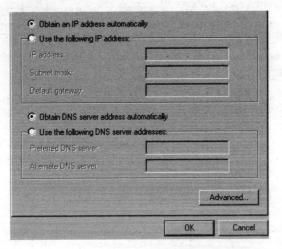

Figure 1.08

5 Make sure that you have selected the radio button to **Obtain an IP address automatically** and that the fields below it for IP address, etc. are blanked out as in Figure 1.08. Click **OK** to confirm any changes you make. This will not require you to restart the PC.

So far we have looked at two PCs – BURGESS and ASIMOV – and, by taking things on trust and following the instructions, we have set them up to 'see' each other. To progress beyond this stage we need to look at some basic networking ideas and terminology.

1.3 Network terminology

Names

Each PC on your network needs a unique name. This is sometimes referred to as the PC's NetBIOS name. It should be no more than 15 characters in length and should not contain spaces, punctuation marks or other special characters. As long as you observe these requirements you can call any PC on your network by any name you like so long as it is unique on your network.

When naming a PC, you can also add a brief description. ASIMOV, in our example is described as 'The one near the window' – a more useful name in a workplace may indicate where the PC is located such as 'Reception area PC' or 'Admin Office PC 2'. These descriptions are simply a matter of human convenience and do not affect the working of your network.

Workgroup

All PCs on your network should be members of the same workgroup. By default this is WORKGROUP for new Windows PCs, but this may have been changed at some point, either by a user or even by a utility such as the Windows XP Internet Connection Sharing Wizard which defaults to the workgroup name MSHOME.

Whatever the default name is you can of course change it to something which suits your organization or tastes. Like the PC's own name, the workgroup name is limited to 15 characters and cannot contain spaces or special characters. All PCs on your network should be members of the same workgroup.

IP address

Even small networks, these days, use the same set of protocols as the Internet. One of these is the Internet Protocol (IP) and this is used to organize numeric addresses for the computers on the network.

If you look again at Figure 1.05 you will see that the PC ASIMOV is also referred to as 169.254.187.195 – this string of numbers in the form *nnn.nnn.nnn.nnn* is the IP address of the PC called ASIMOV. The relationship between a PC's name and its IP address is similar to that of a person's name and their phone number: the number is what makes it possible to run the phone system, the name is easier for humans to remember.

This name and number relationship also holds good for the Internet itself. If you are connected to the net, start a command prompt and PING a URL such as **www.bbc.co.uk** and look at the results.

```
C:\>PING WWW.BBC.CO.UK

Pinging www.bbc.net.UK [212.58.227.77] with 32 bytes of data:

Reply from 212.58.227.77: bytes=32 time=25ms TTL=243
Reply from 212.58.227.77: bytes=32 time=30ms TTL=243
Reply from 212.58.227.77: bytes=32 time=20ms TTL=243
Reply from 212.58.227.77: bytes=32 time=30ms TTL=243
```

Figure 1.09

We'll look at IP addressing schemes in more detail in Chapter 6.

Subnet mask

Just as a full phone number is divided into an area code and the phone number itself, an IP address contains two sets of information: the network address and the host or PC address. The subnet mask is the means by which the network distinguishes between the two.

If we had a telephone number 01879265123 we may, for clarity and ease of use, write this as (01879)265123. By convention, we know that the part of the number which is in brackets is the area code, and the remainder is the phone number itself.

A subnet mask is used in a similar fashion to distinguish between the network part of the IP address and the address of the individual PC on that network.

Given ASIMOV's IP address (above) and the subnet mask 255.255.0.0 we can determine the values of the parts of the address quite easily.

IP Address   169.254.187.195

Subnet mask 255.255.000.000

The part of the full address which corresponds with the 255 values in the subnet mask (169.254) is the network part of the address and the part which corresponds with the 000 values in the subnet mask is the host part of the address. ASIMOV, then, is host (or PC) number 187.195 on the network 169.254.

On the small networks which are the subject of this book you will most commonly come across subnet masks of 255.255.0.0 (Class 'B') and 255.255.255.0 (Class 'C'). Most of the time, Windows organizes the appropriate subnet mask for the IP address system in use.

1.4 Two more commands

We have seen that the PING command can be used to test basic connectivity – to say 'are you there?' to another PC on the network. Two other useful commands are also worth knowing: NET VIEW and IPCONFIG.

NET VIEW

The NET command has many options which need not concern us here, but one of them, NET VIEW gives a listing of the names (and associated comments) on all the PCs attached to your network.

```
C:\>NET VIEW
Server Name              Remark

\\ASIMOV                 The one near the window
\\BURGESS
The command completed successfully.
```

Figure 1.10

Figure 1.10 shows the two PCs attached to our network. The double backslash characters prefixed to the names \\ASIMOV and \\BURGESS indicate that these are PCs on a network. This naming convention is known as the Universal Naming Convention (UNC). It is also used to indicate other resources that are shared on a network.

IPCONFIG

Just as the NET command is concerned with the network, the IPCONFIG command works at the level of the individual PC. Like NET, it has a number of options which do not concern us at present.

Used without options or switches, IPCONFIG reports on the IP configuration of the PC on which it is run.

```
C:\>IPCONFIG

Windows IP Configuration

Ethernet adapter Local Area Connection:

        Connection-specific DNS Suffix  . :
        Autoconfiguration IP Address. . . : 169.254.101.146
        Subnet Mask . . . . . . . . . . . : 255.255.0.0
        Default Gateway . . . . . . . . . :
```

Figure 1.11

Figure 1.11 shows us that the machine on which it has been run has an IP address of 169.254.101.146 (automatically assigned) and a subnet mask of 255.255.0.0. The information about DNS and Default Gateway do not concern us at present.

Help on any Windows topic can be found through the Help and Support services in Windows and the Microsoft website.

For help on commands, open a Command Prompt and type 'help' in the box. This will list all the available commands on the system. In order to list the commands a page at a time, use the *pipe* operator (the vertical bar on the backslash key, next to [Shift]) to send the output through the MORE filter, like this:

HELP | MORE (followed by [Enter]).

To find help on a particular command – usage, options, etc. – type the name of the command followed by a space and the forward slash and question mark characters. For example, to obtain help on IPCONFIG type:

IPCONFIG /? (followed by [Enter])

And if the output is too long, then pipe it through MORE.

Summary

In this chapter we have looked at the basics of linking two PCs to form a small (a very small) network: installing a network adaptor, linking two PCs on a crossover cable and testing the connection.

We have looked at some LAN terminology and introduced some technicalities such as IP addresses etc. We have looked at some diagnostic commands: PING, NET VIEW and IPCONFIG, and seen how to get help on these and other commands.

This chapter has covered a lot of ground in few pages and some of it may look quite complicated at first sight. Like most things in computing, the best way to learn is to have a go. Buy – or even make – a crossover cable and experiment on a pair of PCs – experiment with PC names, workgroup names and the commands that we have looked at. Time spent working though the ideas presented here will be a worthwhile investment before progressing to the rest of the book.

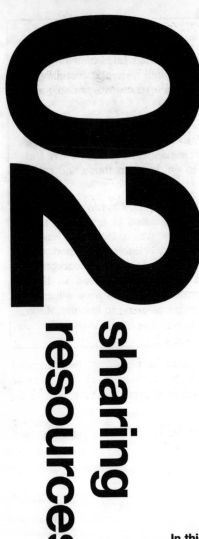

02 sharing resources

In this chapter you will learn:

- how to share a modem
- how to share a printer
- how to share files and manage a shared file store
- about synchronizing files

2.1 Sharing resources

The main reason why most users want a network is the ability to share resources: physical resources such as a printer or modem, or data in the form of files. To do this, you need to have a user account on each of the PCs and it must be password-protected.

Setting up user accounts

Every Windows PC has a special Administrator user account and at least one other user account. Normally, the first user account has Administrator privileges and can carry out administrative tasks such as creating new user accounts or modifying existing accounts.

To make life easier for the home user, Windows does not make it mandatory for user accounts to be password-protected. This is fine for home users, but for an office network you need password-protected accounts. For one thing, it is good practice to have them from the point of view of general security; second, some features of your network may not work properly if user accounts are not password-protected.

As with many administrative tasks in Windows, user account settings can be accessed through the Control Panel. The route to the functions that we need is slightly different in XP and in Vista, but the differences are small.

In **XP** navigate to: **Start > Control Panel > User Accounts** and you will see something like Figure 2.01a.

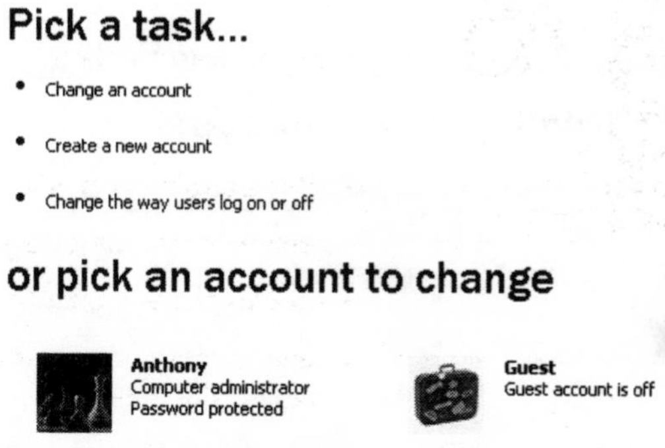

Pick a task...

- Change an account

- Create a new account

- Change the way users log on or off

or pick an account to change

Anthony
Computer administrator
Password protected

Guest
Guest account is off

Figure 2.01a Modifying user accounts in XP.

On a **Vista** system, navigate to **Start > Control Panel > User Accounts and Family Safety > User Accounts** and you will see something like Figure 2.01b.

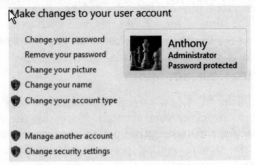

Make changes to your user account

Change your password
Remove your password
Change your picture
Change your name
Change your account type

Manage another account
Change security settings

Anthony
Administrator
Password protected

Figure 2.01b Modifying user accounts in Vista.

To create a new user account in Vista you will need to click on the **Manage another account** option to reach the **Create a new account** option.

These types of minor differences in navigation, naming conventions and appearance between Windows versions are commonplace and something that we all have to live with. The example which follows is based on XP Professional – your system may look slightly different.

Creating a new user in XP

1 Navigate to the screen shown in Figure 2.01a and click on **Create a new account**.

2 Enter the name of the new account in the box:

Name the new account

Type a name for the new account:

Isaac

This name will appear on the Welcome screen and on the Start menu.

Figure 2.02

3 Click **Next**.

4 Choose the account type – *Computer Administrator* or *Limited* then click the **Create Account** button.

Note that the new account is not password-protected by default. To remedy this:

1 Navigate to the **User Account** applet in the **Control Panel** and click on it.

2 Click on the icon for the new account. You will be presented with the choices to either change the name of the account or to create a password.

3 Click on **Create a Password**. This will present you with the dialog box shown in Figure 2.03.

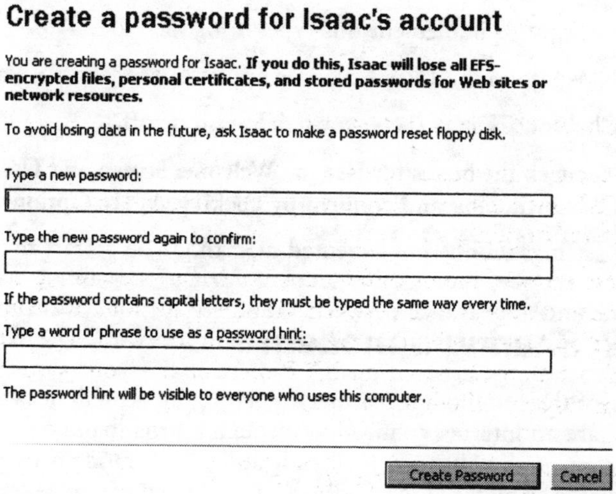

Create a password for Isaac's account

You are creating a password for Isaac. **If you do this, Isaac will lose all EFS-encrypted files, personal certificates, and stored passwords for Web sites or network resources.**

To avoid losing data in the future, ask Isaac to make a password reset floppy disk.

Type a new password:

Type the new password again to confirm:

If the password contains capital letters, they must be typed the same way every time.

Type a word or phrase to use as a password hint:

The password hint will be visible to everyone who uses this computer.

Create Password   Cancel

Figure 2.03

4 Read the instructions on screen, allocate the new password and optional hint.

5 Click on **Create Password**.

6 Windows will now report the account as Password-protected.

7 Click the **Close** button at the top right of the window to return to the main Control Panel.

All of your users will now be required to log on to the system by entering a password at either the default Welcome screen or the more formal logon box shown in Figure 2.04.

Figure 2.04

If you want to implement this type of logon:

1 Navigate to the **User Accounts** applet in the **Control Panel.**

2 Click on **Change the way users log on or off.**

3 Uncheck the boxes for **Use the Welcome Screen** and **Use Fast User Switching** and confirm by clicking **Apply Options.**

The settings will be implemented next time you restart the PC.

2.2 Sharing a modem

One of the commonest reasons for setting up a small network is to share an Internet connection through a broadband or dial up modem. You will need to install and test a modem to work through the material that follows – if you need guidance on how to do this refer to the modem manufacturer's documentation or *Teach Yourself Home PC Maintenance and Networking.*

In the example which follows we will look at the process of sharing a modem which has been installed on an XP Professional system – the Internet PC – with a second PC running XP or Vista – the client PC.

In outline the process is:

1 Attach and install the modem to the Internet PC.

2 Run the **Network Setup Wizard** on the Internet PC. The wizard will prompt you to make a floppy disk to transfer the settings to the client PC – don't bother with this.

3 Reboot the client PC if necessary.

Set up the Internet PC

On the XP machine (that has the modem attached):

1 Navigate to **Control Panel** and click on the applet for the **Network Setup Wizard**.

2 Click **Next** at the welcome screen. Read the comments and, if necessary, review the checklist for creating a network. Click **Next** to continue.

3 Select the **Connects directly to the Internet** option, then click **Next**.

4 Highlight your modem as in Figure 2.05.

Figure 2.05

5 Click **Next**. You will be given the opportunity to change the name of the PC or to change its description. Make any changes that you want, then click **Next** again.

6 The wizard proposes MSHOME as the name of your workgroup. Change this to your chosen workgroup name. In this example it is HAVEN.

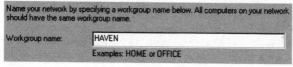

Figure 2.06

7 At the next screen, accept the default action to enable file and print sharing. Click on **Next,** then **Next** again to apply the new network settings. Windows will now spend a couple of minutes setting up the shared connection.

Behind the scenes, Windows is assigning a static IP address of 192.168.0.1 for the Internet PC and is setting up a DHCP server which will allocate IP addresses to other PCs that want to connect to it to share the Internet connection. You don't really need to know about this – you can just treat it as magic if you like – but if you know how something works rather than how to work it you have a lot more control over your computing environment. DHCP – the Dynamic Host Configuration Protocol – is discussed in more detail in Chapter 6, *Expanding your network*.

8 When the Wizard has completed its work select the **Just finish the wizard** option.

9 Click **Next**, then click **Finish** at the final screen.

Setting up the client PC

If the client PC has been set up with default settings there will be little, if anything, to do. The client will obtain its IP address and other settings from the DHCP server running on the Internet PC. Click on the web browser and see if you can connect to the Internet. If you can – fine. If not, reboot the client PC.

Vista client

When the client restarts, if it is running Vista you will probably see a message like the one in Figure 2.07.

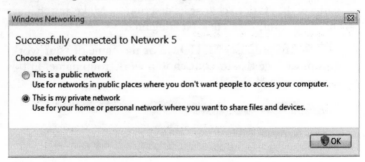

Figure 2.07

Select the **Private network** option and click **OK**. Vista will set up your default Desktop as usual, and you can check your new connection by clicking on your browser to connect to the Internet. You can also look at your new connection through **Control Panel > Network and Internet > Network Center**.

Figure 2.08

XP client

If you are running XP on the client PC there is no boot time message. Either it works or it doesn't. Check your connection by trying to connect to the Internet with your browser or start a command prompt and PING an Internet site such as one of the major search engines like Google or Altavista. If it works, fine. If not, the problem is probably with your network settings.

2.3 Network connection settings

Whether you are using XP or Vista on the client PC, the connection must be set up to obtain an IP address automatically. This is the default for both XP and Vista but the settings may have changed without your knowing, so here's how to check.

Windows Vista

1 Navigate to **Control Panel > View network status and tasks.**

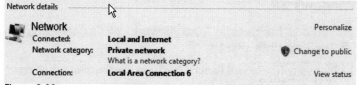

Figure 2.09

2 Click the **View status** link.

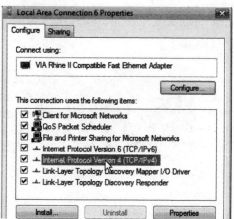

Figure 2.10

3 Highlight the **Internet Protocol Version 4** entry in the list, then click **Properties**.

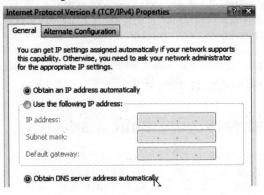

Figure 2.11

Figure 2.11 shows that this connection is set to the default value of **Obtain an IP address automatically,** which is what we want.

Windows XP

The process for checking your network connection settings in XP is essentially similar.

1 Navigate to **Control Panel > Network Connections** then right-click on the connection that you want to investigate (for most users there will probably only be one).

2 Click on the **Properties** entry in the context menu and select Internet Protocol (TCP/IP) from the list.

3 Click **Properties**.

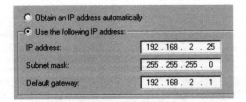

Figure 2.12

In this instance the system has been given a static IP address which is not what we want at present for this connection.

To fix this problem:

1 Select **Obtain an IP address automatically**.

2 Click **OK** to make the changes permanent. There is no need to reboot the machine after doing this.

2.4 Sharing a printer

Sharing a printer is something that most people will want to implement on their network. On a small Windows network this can be achieved by setting up a Share on a locally installed printer on one of the PCs. In this example, we will look at sharing an existing local printer on an XP system with a network connection to a Vista machine.

To see the installed printers on the XP machine, navigate to **Start > Printers and Faxes**. This will show you a list of installed printers – in this example a single printer, an Epson Stylus Photo 890.

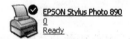

Figure 2.13

Figure 2.13 shows that the printer is installed, is ready to accept jobs and has no jobs in the queue. It's still not a bad idea, though, to print a test page at this point just to be sure that all is well.

Creating the share

1 Right-click on the printer and select **Properties** from the menu.

2 Select the **Sharing** tab.

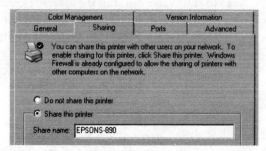

Figure 2.14

3 Select **Share this printer** and give it a meaningful name.

4 Click **OK** to finish.

Windows now displays the printer icon with a hand underneath it to indicate that the printer is shared.

Figure 2.15

Connecting from Vista

Having created the printer share on the XP system we can now link to it across the network from the Vista machine. To do this:

1 Open the Vista Control Panel and click on the link for **Printers** in the **Hardware and Sound** section.

2 Select **Add Printer** from the menu bar, then check the radio button to search for a network printer.

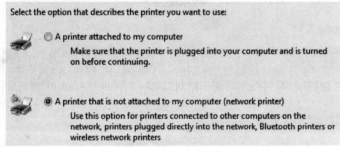

Figure 2.16

3 Click **Next** to start. You can stop the search, or if it fails you can click the link **The printer I am looking for is not on this list**, then choose **Select a printer on the network by name**.

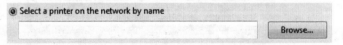

Figure 2.17

4 Click **Browse**.

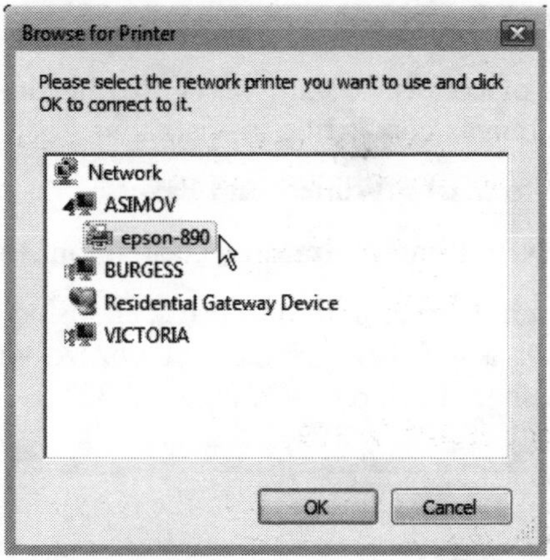

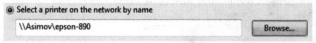

Figure 2.18

5 Expand the view of the network until you can see the printer on the XP machine, then click **OK**. This will plug in the network address of the host PC \\ASIMOV and the name of the printer share, epson-890.

Figure 2.19

6 To continue with the printer installation click **Next**. Vista will display a warning message. Click **Yes** to continue. Vista will complete the connection and confirm this.

Figure 2.20

7 By default the newly installed printer will be made the default and Vista will print a test page. Note that the name displayed in the figure is the printer name rather than the share name which you gave to it.

8 Click **Next**, and Vista will confirm the installation of the new printer and it will be shown in the Printers section of the Vista Control Panel.

Connecting from XP

The process of connecting an XP PC to the shared printer is almost the same as connecting in Vista.

1 Navigate to **Start > Printers and Faxes.**

2 Run the New Printer wizard by clicking on **Add a printer.**

3 Step though the stages of the wizard, choosing the options to browse for a network printer. The wizard will display the available shared printer as in Figure 2.21.

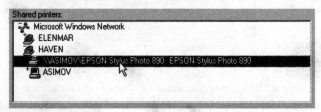

Shared printers:

-- Microsoft Windows Network
  ⊞ ELENMAR
  ⊞ HAVEN
    \\ASIMOV\EPSON Stylus Photo 890   EPSON Stylus Photo 890
  + ASIMOV

Figure 2.21

4 Highlight the printer and click **Next**. Set this as the default at the next screen if you wish to, click **Next**, then **Finish**.

2.5 Sharing files

Sharing files between Windows computers is much the same as sharing any other resource – set up the share on the object that you want to make available, by right-clicking, then enabling sharing.

Sharing a folder in XP

1 Select or create, a folder that you want to share.

2 Right-click on the folder icon, then click on the **Sharing and security** item in the context menu or select **Properties**, then select the **Sharing** tab. Whichever route you choose you will be presented with the dialog box shown in Figure 2.22.

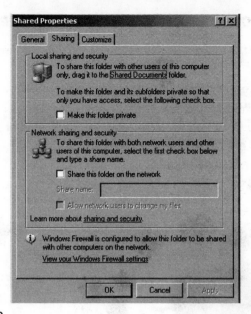

Figure 2.22

3 To share the folder, tick the box labelled **Share this folder on the network**. This will enable read-only access to the contents of the folder and of any subfolders. It also allows you to make two other choices: the ability to allow full access (read/write) and to give the share a name which is different from the folder name. This is the one which will be seen by users who connect to it over the network. Tick the required boxes and give the share a name, then click **OK**.

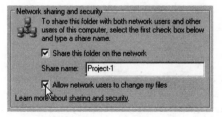

Figure 2.23

In this instance, a folder called *Shared* has been made available with read/write access under the share name *Project-1*.

2.6 How to access a shared folder

To access the folder from elsewhere on the network using an XP machine:

1 Click on **My Network Places** then choose **Add a network place** to start the **Add Network Place Wizard**.

2 Accept the Windows defaults by clicking **Next** until you reach the screen with the **Browse** button.

3 Click **Browse** and navigate to the shared folder on the remote PC.

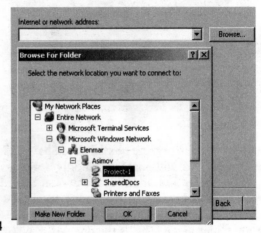

Figure 2.24

4 Highlight the folder you want to connect to and click **OK**. Windows will provide a default name for your new network place. You can change this to something more meaningful if you wish.

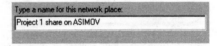

Figure 2.25

By default, the new network place will be opened when you click **OK**. It will also appear in My Network Places. If you intend to use this folder frequently, right-click on the Network Place and use the **Send to** option to create a Desktop shortcut. If you wish you can then rename your shortcut. As an alternative to the procedures outlined above, you can start by creating a new shortcut. Right-click on an empty piece of Desktop and choose **New > Shortcut**, then browse to the shared folder from there.

Figure 2.26

This method of creating a Desktop shortcut also works in Vista.

Sharing a folder in Vista

The process of setting up a shared folder in Vista is much the same as in XP, though it gives you a little more control over who has access.

To set up the share, right-click on the folder icon and select **Share** from the context menu. You will be presented with a screen like the one in Figure 2.27.

Click the tab at the top of the box to drop down a list of users with accounts on the PC. You may select individuals by name, everyone in the list, or create a new account with **Create a new user**. When you have decided which users are to have access to

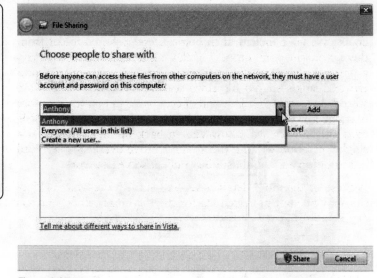

Figure 2.27

the shared folder, you can assign each user one of three different levels of access:

+ **Reader** – has read-only access to the folder and its contents, including subfolders and files;

+ **Contributor** – has read-only access to all files and can create their own files which they can then modify or delete;

+ **Co-owner** – has the same full read/write/modify rights as the owner of the folder.

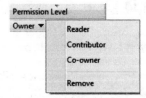

Figure 2.28

Settings for each user (or group) are set through this list and confirmed by clicking **Share** at the bottom of the screen.

To connect to the shared folder from another PC on the network, browse to it by the methods described earlier in this chapter, i.e. add a network place (XP) or create a shortcut (XP or Vista) and navigate to the target folder.

2.7 Setting up a shared file store

So far, we have looked at the file-sharing possibilities of Windows from the point of view of sharing folders or files for (say) a particular project. We can, however, use these capabilities to create a single shared file store so that all user data files are stored on a single PC. This will of course mean that the file store machine must always be available. However, using a central file store in this way will allow you to back up all user files in a single operation without the administrative overheads involved in setting up and administering a client/server network.

Because of the more detailed access controls available in Vista this may be your preferred PC for the shared file store, but this can be implemented equally well on an XP machine.

Creating and sharing the shared data folder

This is a three-stage process:

1 Navigate to a suitable storage area on the server PC. Create a folder called (say) *User-Data* and set up a share on it.

2 Create a subfolder for each user and assign the necessary permissions.

3 Redirect each user's *My Documents* folder to point to the shared file store.

In this example, we will create a shared folder for all users and a subfolder for the user Anthony on a Vista PC. We will then redirect Anthony's **My Documents** folder on an XP machine to point to this location.

On the file store PC

To create the new shared area on the file store PC (running Vista):

1 Click on **Start > Computer**, then click on the drive icon for the C: drive.

2 Right-click on an empty area of the right-hand pane to open the context menu and select **New > Folder**.

3 Rename the new folder *User-Data*.

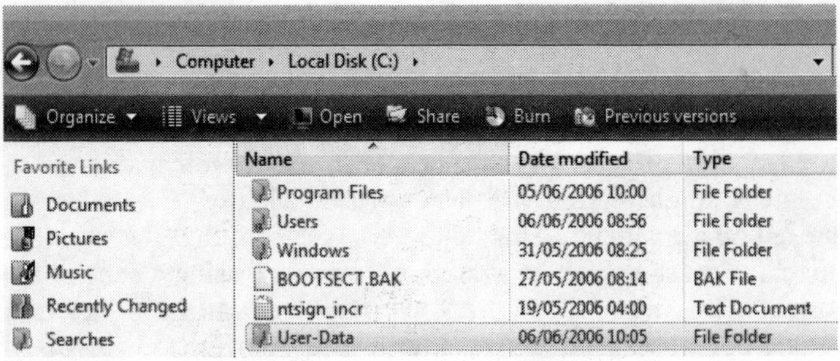

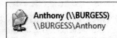

Figure 2.29

4 Click on the *User-Data* folder.

5 Create a new folder inside *User-Data* for the user Anthony.

6 Create a share on this folder and assign full rights to the user Anthony.

When you click on the **Share** button Vista will confirm the network path to the new folder.

Anthony (\\BURGESS)
\\BURGESS\Anthony

Figure 2.30

On the workstation PC

Obviously, you have to be logged on to the (XP) workstation PC as the user whose name you have used to set up the share – in this case, Anthony.

To redirect the user's My Documents:

1 Right-click on the **My Documents** icon and select **Properties** from the context menu. This will show the current location of the My Documents folder as in Figure 2.31.

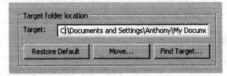

Figure 2.31

2 Click **Move**, then navigate to the folder where you want the documents to be stored.

Figure 2.32

3   Click **OK** to confirm this new location. You will be given the
option to move files to the new location if you want to.

When you have finished, Windows will show the new location
as in Figure 2.33.

Figure 2.33

Note that you have the option to **Find Target** (in effect a shortcut
to it), to **Move** to a different destination, or to **Restore Default**.
The default location for *My Documents* is usually *C:\Documents
and settings\username\My Documents*. The ability to restore
default values in this way is useful – it means that you can experiment, knowing that you can undo your changes if necessary.

Other permutations of XP and Vista

The example that we have worked through assumed that you
will be connecting an XP workstation to a Vista file store. However, you don't have to do it this way. If the workstation PC is
running Vista, the procedure for redirecting a user's *Documents*
folder is the same.

◆ Right-click on the *Documents* folder, and choose **Properties > Locations > Move** then follow the instructions for XP.

You can also, of course, use an XP machine for your shared file store, though you will have slightly less control over access rights than when using Vista.

2.8 Managing the file store

The most important thing about your file store machine is that it must always be available for the workstations to be able to access their files. That is as simple as making sure that it's the first machine to be turned on at the start of the working day and the last one to be turned off. If your file store PC is also your gateway to the Internet there may be a case for leaving it on permanently.

The main advantage of having a central file store of this type is that you can back up everyone's files in a single job. Where the total size of files amounts to less than the capacity of a CD or DVD disk this can be achieved simply by burning the whole of the User-Data folder (along with its subfolders) to a writable disk. Backups are examined more fully in Chapter 7, *Fault tolerance and disaster recovery*.

The main disadvantage of a central file store is that it places a lot of eggs in the same basket. If the hard disk on the file store machine fails or it becomes corrupted or is subjected to a virus attack, then everyone is in trouble. Risks can be minimized and managed – Chapter 7 looks at some of the means of avoiding equipment failures. Security, in the broader sense is the subject of Chapter 9, *Internet and e-mail* and Chapter 14, *Security*.

2.9 Synchronizing files

When you attach a PC – laptop or desktop, wired or wireless – to a shared folder, you need to make sure that you are working with the latest versions of your files. Where the connection is permanent, there is only one set of files – the ones in the shared store – so synchronization is not a problem and can be disabled to boost performance. Where a PC – typically a laptop using a wireless connection – is used to work on files both at the office and away from it, then you need to be sure that you are working with the latest version. For example, if you wrote a letter at the office and saved it to the shared file store, then edited it at home on your laptop, you would want the new version available on both systems. This is achieved through file synchronization.

In XP:

1 Navigate to **Control Panel > Folder Options** and select the **Offline Files** tab.

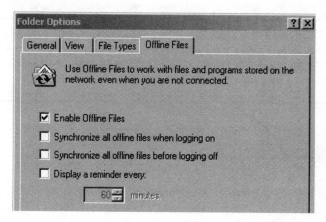

Figure 2.34

2 Enable synchronization by ticking the box to **Enable Offline Files** then click **Apply**. You can also control whether to synchronize when logging on or logging off (or both, if you wish). Make your choices and save them with **Apply**.

In Vista, the basic setup is even easier:

1 Navigate to your shared folder over your network.

2 Right-click on the shared folder name and select the **Always available offline** option from the context menu.

For advanced synchronization options in Vista, there is an **Offline Files** applet in Control Panel.

The synchronization facilities provided by Windows are probably sufficient for most users, but if you want something more sophisticated there are many third-party utilities. A Web search on 'Windows file synchronization' will give you several options.

Summary

In this chapter we have looked at the practicalities of sharing resources between two PCs running some combination of Windows XP and Windows Vista operating systems. We have seen how to share a modem, a printer and files between password-protected user accounts.

The examples have been taken from the smallest possible network – two PCs – and have considered both XP and Vista operating systems for the tasks involved. The principles outlined in this chapter can be applied to networks with more than two PCs, though it should be noted that the Home editions of Windows – both XP and Vista – are restricted in some of their networking capabilities.

03 cables and connectors

In this chapter you will learn:

- the main cable types used in small networks

- the connectors used in small networks

- the tools and techniques used with cabling

3.1 Network cables

The most frequently used cable type for small networks is the type known as *unshielded twisted pair* – usually abbreviated to UTP. This cable type was originally used for telephony and comes in several categories which are defined by the American National Standards Institute (ANSI).

For networking purposes, the key characteristics are the speed at which the cable can carry a signal – its *bandwidth* – and the maximum length of cable that you may have between the PCs on your network. The speed of communications is measured in millions of bits (megabits) per second – usually abbreviated to Mbps. (Note, the lower-case 'b' which indicates 'bits' rather than the upper-case 'B' which would indicate 'Bytes'). The distance between machines is specified in metres.

The most frequently used cable types for a modern small network are:

Category	Capacity	Segment length
5	10–100 Mbps	100 metres (328 feet)
5e	100 Mbps	100 metres (328 feet)
6	1000 Mbps (1 Gbps)	100 metres (328 feet)

All of these cable types use the RJ45 connector to connect to network devices such as the PCs on the network or other networking components such as hubs, switches or routers.

The performance of a network cabling system will depend on the capacity of the cables, the connectors and the quality of workmanship used to put them together. For example, a category 6 cable, using all four of its twisted pairs and the correct RJ45 connector, will deliver a performance rating of 1000 Mbps – 'Gigabit Ethernet'. However, for the network as a whole to be classified as Category 6, all components must be able to interconnect and test at this speed.

Selecting a cable category for your network is simple – buy the best that you can afford. In practice, you will upgrade individual components such as the PCs you are using, or their network cards, several times in the lifetime of your cable installation. Even if you don't plan on using the full gigabit performance available from category 6 cabling immediately, installing it *could* give you a degree of future proofing of your investment of time and money.

Inside the twisted pair cable

A twisted pair cable has an outer cover – usually PVC – and inside there are four colour coded pairs of wire which are twisted around one another as shown in Figure 3.01.

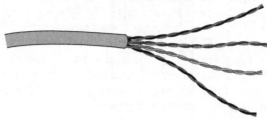

Figure 3.01

The twists in the cable pairs are necessary to reduce electrical cross-talk between them and to maintain signal quality. Each pair has a different number of twists per inch to reduce cross-talk between the pairs. It is important to take this into account when making up cables.

The cable pairs are colour coded: Blue, Brown, Green and Orange, and each solid colour is twisted with a corresponding striped wire so that they are paired Blue/Blue and White, Brown/Brown and White and so on.

Category 5 and 5e cables only use four of the available wires, whereas category 6 uses all eight. Even if you are using less than the full capacity of category 6 – Gigabit Ethernet – you should make sure that all eight wires connect properly. Settling for anything less is a false economy which will cause you problems in the future when you upgrade the rest of your network.

3.2 Connectors

RJ45

The RJ45 is the connector which is used to connect category 5 and 6 cables to network devices such as the network cards on a

PC or a router, switch or hub. The *RJ* indicates that the connector is a *Registered Jack* – a classification which is used in the US for connectors. The US telephone connector is an *RJ11* connector, similar in appearance but smaller. This is frequently used as a connector on modem cables even in the UK where the phone connector is different.

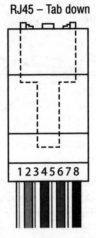

RJ45 – Tab down

1 2 3 4 5 6 7 8

Figure 3.02 The RJ45 is viewed with the securing tab facing away and the line numbers are labelled 1–8 from left to right. These correspond to the individual colour coded inner strands of the category 5/6 cable.

Line jack/faceplate/surface box

These provide a telephone style socket on the wall. They can be flush mounted (i.e. you cut a hole in the wall into which the connector is fitted) or surface mounted.

Fixing may be through a self-adhesive back to the box or it may be done using plugs and screws. To some extent, your choice in this will be a matter of personal preference and may depend on the type of wall you are fixing to.

Patch panel

If you are connecting more than two computers you will need to use a device such as a hub or switch at the centre of your network. You can attach your category 5/6 cables directly to such a device, but it may be good practice to use an intermediate connection known as a patch panel. Larger patch panels are usually 19 inches (48 cm) wide – the standard for most rack-mounted network equipment. Figure 3.03 shows a smaller panel intended for wall mounting which is suitable for smaller networks

The patch panel has connectors at the back which are similar to those inside a wall-mounted connector, and provide a permanent connection for the cable end. This means that you have network connection points around your office connected to the patch panel. The front of the patch panel has standard sockets which take an RJ45. Connections from the patch panel ports to those of the hub or switch are then implemented using short (typically a metre in length) pieces of category 5/6 cable with a standard RJ45 at each end. These are known as *patch cables*.

The mechanics of the patch panel arrangement are rather like an old-fashioned telephone exchange – you can create or remove any connection by moving the ends of the patch cables between ports on the panel and your hub, switch or router without affecting any other connections or modifying your main cabling setup. Providing that your wall sockets are numbered and the connections on the patch panel have corresponding numbers, you can 'patch' or modify any connection from a single point on the panel.

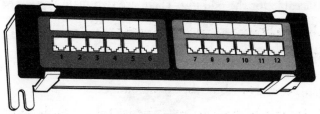

Figure 3.03 Single outlet faceplate/module for surface mounting.

3.3 Tools

Obviously, when you are cabling a network – even a small one – you will need various general purpose tools: wire strippers, a sharp knife, screwdrivers, tape and so forth. In addition, you will need a *crimping tool* and a *punch-down* tool.

Crimping tool

Like most hand tools, crimping tools are available as top-of-the-range professional equipment with interchangeable jaws for different applications or in basic versions suitable for occasional use. All that is required for our purposes is a basic crimper which will handle RJ45 connectors. It is useful to have one which has a wire cutter and/or an insulation stripper built in, but these are not essential.

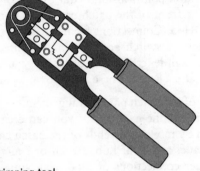

Figure 3.04 A crimping tool.

Punch-down tool

These may be professional quality or they may be cheap and serviceable for the odd job. There are two main types – Krone and 110 – you will need to buy the type required to connect to the outlets and to the patch panel. Some patch panels are compatible with both types of punch-down tool.

Figure 3.05 A punch-down tool.

Cable tester

Probably the most expensive tool in the toolbox will be a cable tester. The top of the range models can cost several hundred pounds and are used by network professionals on big network installations where advanced diagnostic capabilities are needed. However, for the small network all that is required is something that can test for basic connectivity, i.e. one that can test category 5/6 cables, though most can be used for other cable types as well. Prices are typically in double (rather than treble) figures.

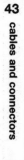

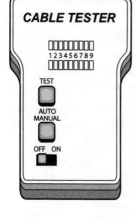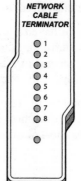

Figure 3.06 A typical two-part cable tester which is capable of testing various cable types over a range of 1,000 feet.

3.4 Techniques

If you haven't done it before, putting an RJ45 on both ends of a category 5 cable or wiring a faceplate can be difficult. The key to success is to work methodically and to accept that you will probably get it wrong at your first, second, or even third try. Before you start, make sure that you have plenty of RJ45 connectors because they cannot be re-used. When they are crimped onto the end of the cable, the block that secures the cable is forced down by the crimping tool. This cannot be reversed, so if you get it wrong you will have to cut a fresh end on your cable and fit a *new* RJ45. If you do a few practice runs with two-metre lengths, then you can always recycle your failures as patch cables later.

It may also be a good idea to use a known good cable to test your test meter before you start.

Fitting an RJ45

To do this you will need a crimping tool to secure the RJ45 plug in place and a means of stripping the outer insulation from the cable – this may be built into the crimping tool, or it can be a cable stripper or a sharp knife. You do not have to remove the outer insulating layer from the inner strands of the cable. You will also need a cable tester to check the quality of your work.

If you haven't made up a network cable before, make sure that you have sufficient spare cable and RJ45 connectors to allow for several mistakes. Making up network cables is a fiddly job and most of us make a mess of it at our first few attempts.

Note: there are two different standards for fitting an RJ45 connector and these are described later. The example which follows uses the T568B standard for the cable layout.

1　Remove 2 inches (5 cm) of the outer layer of insulation.

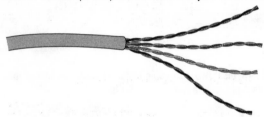

Figure 3.07

2　Separate the pairs and untwist them. Make sure that you don't allow them to untwist back into the covered part of the cable – this can impair network performance.

3　Arrange the now untwisted wires like this:

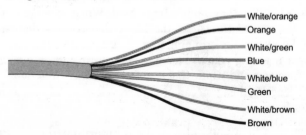

Figure 3.08

4 Trim the wires to ½" (12 mm) from the end of the outer insulation. Most crimping tools have a cutter built into the handle for this. Make sure that you have a clean, straight cut.

5 Push the wires into the RJ45. Make sure they are fully inserted and that the outer layer of insulation is well inside it.

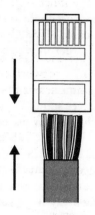

Figure 3.09

6 Put the RJ45 into the jaw of the crimper.

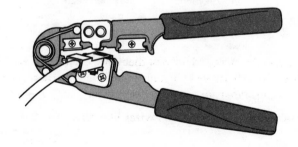

Figure 3.10

7 Check that the cable is still properly aligned and fully inserted into the RJ45. Crimp the RJ45 end.

8 Repeat steps 1 to 7 on the other end of the cable.

9 Test your cable with a cable tester.

Note: although you need to remove the insulation from the outer layer of category 5/6 cable, you don't need to do this with the inner, colour coded, strands.

3.5 The T568A and T568B standards

As if life isn't complicated enough, there are two different standards for wiring an Ethernet cable – T568A and T568B. The difference between them is the order in which the wires are fitted in the RJ45/faceplate/patch panel.

Obviously, if you want to connect to an existing network you will need to stick with whatever standard you have inherited. If you are starting from scratch you may use either, so long as you are consistent. Most people use the T568B standard, though the T568A standard is preferred by the US government. Whichever convention you choose, remember that the pin numbers and the diagrams assume that you are looking at the RJ45 connector with the retaining clip facing away from you.

Pin number	Colour – T568A	Colour – T568B
1	White/Green	White/Orange
2	Green	Orange
3	White/Orange	White/Green
4	Blue	Blue
5	White/Blue	White/Blue
6	Orange	Green
7	White/Brown	White/Brown
8	Brown	Brown

Note: category 5 and 5e installations only use pins 1, 2, 3 and 6. Category 6 uses all of them so even if it isn't strictly necessary now, it is good practice to make sure that all eight lines are working properly.

Another cable type which you may find useful is a crossover cable in which send and receive lines are crossed so that you can connect two computers without using a hub or switch. You can buy these ready-made, but if you have a drum of cable, some RJ45s and the necessary tools for the remainder of your cabling project you can easily make your own crossover cables.

3.6 Making a crossover cable

Follow the instructions for an RJ45, but arrange the pairs thus:

Pin number	Colour – End 1	Colour – End 2
1	White/Orange	White/Green
2	Orange	Green
3	White/Green	White/Orange
4	Blue	White/Brown
5	White/Blue	Brown
6	Green	Orange
7	White/Brown	Blue
8	Brown	White/Blue

This is based on the T568B standard and, since all pairs are crossed, will function as a crossover cable on both 100 Mbps and 1 Gigabit connections.

Wiring a faceplate/patch panel

To wire a faceplate or patch panel connection (Figures 3.11 and 3.12), prepare the cable as for an RJ45 – i.e. strip the outer layer of insulation and straighten and arrange the twisted pairs. Most panels/plates are colour coded to show which strand goes where.

To connect the cable, pull each coloured strand over the appropriate connector on the back of the plate or panel and push it firmly into place with the punch down tool. Keep the outer cover of the cable within a quarter of an inch of where the inner wires separate to their pin locations. The punch-down tool pushes the wire between the metal pins on the block, removing the outer skin of insulation to give an electrical contact, and trims the excess wire from the end.

Test the connection with your cable tester and label each end of the connection with a unique number so that faceplate 1 corresponds with port 1 on the patch panel, and so on.

The practicalities of cabling

If you only want to connect two PCs in the same room, all you will need is a crossover cable of the right length to join the two. Make or buy a cable of the correct length and connect the two

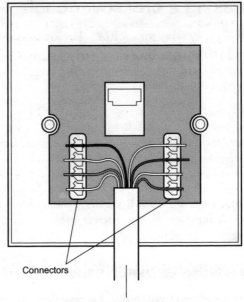

Connectors

Category 5/6 cable

Figure 3.11 The back of a typical faceplate.

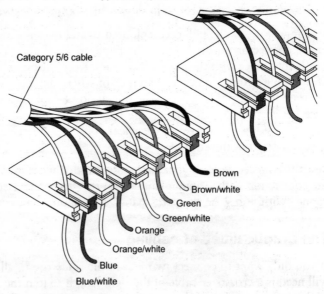

Category 5/6 cable

Brown
Brown/white
Green
Green/white
Orange
Orange/white
Blue
Blue/white

Figure 3.12 The back of a typical patch panel.

machines. Obviously, you will need to take into account Health and Safety considerations as well as the safety of the cable itself. Don't, for example, run your cable anywhere where people can trip over it. You should also avoid running cable where it may be subject to any form of electromagnetic interference from, say, mains electricity cables.

An obvious solution is to use some form of trunking to carry the cable from point to point. Trunking can vary in size, price and material but for the small network all that is required is mini trunking. This is rectangular in section and can be bought by the metre. It can be cut to length with a hacksaw and there are stand-ard joining pieces for turning corners, etc. Some types of trunking are self-adhesive, while others need to be fixed to the wall with screws and plugs.

3.7 Organizing yourself (and others)

If you want to connect more than a couple of PCs, or if you are going to need access to more than one room or office, you will need to organize yourself and your colleagues (who may not be involved in the installation) to minimize the disruption of nor-mal work activities. The problems are not so much technical IT ones as those associated with building work. You will need to move machines and desks, drill holes, fix trunking, pull cables. You will need a storage area for tools and equipment: lengths of trunking, cable drums and so forth. None of this is conducive to the smooth running of day-to-day office work and/or dealing with customers. Ideally, you should have a free day – or even a weekend – when no other work is being done to implement your network infrastructure, but if this isn't possible you should have a timetable for the work and explain to other staff what is being done, when, and how it will affect them. People will generally put up with quite a lot provided they feel that they have been consulted and are kept informed of what is going on.

For anything other than the smallest of installations you must have a thought-out network plan and all the necessary tools and equipment needed to implement it. Chapter 5, *Planning your network* looks at this in more detail.

Health and Safety

Health and Safety considerations are important in any workplace and you should be careful to observe any laws or regulations which apply to the location where you are working. Regulations vary between countries and states and are updated from time to time – if you have any doubts, ask.

In particular, you may be working with sharp cutting tools and drilling or sawing through walls and partitions and creating dust and debris. Have a vacuum cleaner on hand, pick up off-cuts and rubbish and dispose of them properly, have face masks if you are going to produce significant amounts of dust. Check that the First Aid box is properly stocked and that there is someone who can use its contents appropriately in the event of an accident. Common sense precautions, like wearing suitable gloves or a face mask will all reduce the probability of accidents and the severity of the outcome if an accident occurs. Depending on the scale of the operations and the nature of the workplace, it may even be wise to check with your insurers about your cover in the event of an accident.

Building regulations

Like Health and Safety laws, building regulations vary from place to place and from time to time. For example, if you are planning on pulling any of your network cable through a ventilation duct or a suspended ceiling space you may be required to use 'plenum grade' cable. This is normal category 5/6 cable which has been constructed with a flame-retardant surface which is slower to combust in the event of a building fire and which does not give off toxic fumes if it *does* catch fire. A phone call, or an e-mail to your local authority before you start work could save you time and money in the long run.

Marking out cable runs and fixing points

You will probably have chosen a lockable room or cupboard – maybe even the cupboard under the stairs – as the central point where your network cables will attach to a patch panel or workgroup switch, hub, or router.

Starting from this point:

+ Measure and mark the route that each cable will take from patch panel to wall plate, paying particular attention to where the cable will pass though walls or ceilings.

+ Make sure that your network cable is well away from any other cables – especially mains power cables – which may be a source of electromagnetic interference.

+ Check that the total cable length will not be more than 100 metres – this is the maximum *total* distance so include a few feet in your calculations to allow for patch cables between PC and wall plate at one end, and patch panel and switch, hub or router at the other. You should also have a couple of metres of slack in the cable – it is good practice to leave a service coil near the end of the cable to allow for later changes.

Remember – 'measure twice and cut once' is the golden rule for everything you do when cabling.

Pulling cable

With your cable runs marked out and the necessary holes cut or drilled, it is time to physically pull the cable through the runs.

1 Start by fixing a label to the end of the cable on the drum. This should indicate the room and the connection number where it will be routed. For example, the cable that will terminate at faceplate 2 in the Reception area could be marked **Reception – 2**, or the one that will terminate at faceplate 1 in Room 5 could be marked **5–1**. Whatever convention you adopt, you need to be sure that each cable can be uniquely identified.

2 With your cable end appropriately labelled, feed the cable through the chosen run. The mechanics of this will depend on your circumstances. You can, for example, tape the end of your cable to a spare piece of trunking or even a broom handle to push it though a ceiling space, or drop it through a cavity wall and 'fish' for it where cable is run between floors. Common sense and ingenuity are you best allies in this task and, although it doesn't feature in most lists of useful tools, a

wire coat hanger can be really useful. Whatever you do *don't force anything*. A cable which has been stretched or kinked may not work at all, or worse, it could be the source of hard-to-trace intermittent faults for months to come.

3 Now that your cable is in place, label the end which is still attached to the drum so that both ends of the cable have corresponding labels. With both labels fixed, cut the end of the cable from the drum end. Make sure that you have enough free cable that you can attach it to the patch panel or switch/hub/router later on. A few feet of cable wasted in this way is negligible in terms of cost and can be left as a service coil or trimmed later.

Repeat these procedures for each planned network connection.

Trunking and faceplates

It should go without saying that trunking should be of sufficient size to accommodate all of the planned cables. Whether you are using a self-adhesive type or one which fixes to the wall with screws, mark its intended position carefully before fixing. A spirit level and a builder's square can be useful in getting this right.

Where faceplates are surface mounted, drill and plug any fixing points and offer up the boxes to check for accuracy. Flush mounted faceplates need to be similarly checked. Repeat this for each planned connection point.

Once you have cables, trunking and faceplates where they should be, the messiest part of the job is done. If you haven't already done so, this is an ideal time to clean and tidy all of the areas affected by your work.

Connecting and testing

Using the tools and techniques outlined on page 47 under the heading *Wiring a faceplate/patch panel*, connect each cable to the back of the faceplate and fix the faceplate to the wall. At the patch panel end punch down the connectors at the back of the patch panel. It makes life easier if you wire the patch panel in logical order. Exactly how you do this is your decision, but if you have a numbering system for your outlets/faceplates that reflects room numbers and connection numbers 1.1, 1.2, 1.3 ... 5.1, 5.2 and so on, then you can arrange your connections on the back of the patch panel in this order from left to right.

In order to test the connections, use your cable tester according to the manufacturer's instructions. Connect the two parts of the tester to the two (labelled) ends of the cable to be tested and test for connectivity of all wires. As each connection tests as OK check it off on a list of connection numbers.

Summary

In this chapter we have looked at the practical aspects of implementing a structured cabling system for a small workplace LAN within a single building.

The cable types, connectors and tools described are all readily available industry standard kit:

- Category 5/6 cable
- RJ45 connectors
- Line jacks/faceplates
- Patch panel
- Crimping tool
- Punch-down tool
- Cable tester

It may be useful to read this chapter in conjunction with Chapter 5, *Planning your network* and Chapter 6 *Expanding your network*.

04 wireless networks

In this chapter you will learn:

- how to set up an ad hoc wireless connection
- how to set up a wireless access point
- how to secure a wireless network

4.1 Why wireless?

Wireless networks offer several advantages over their wired coun-terparts. They are easy to set up, flexible in their use and can be deployed where cabling is not feasible. For example, cabling may be inappropriate in some buildings for aesthetic reasons or there may be an awkwardly placed office at the back of the premises or a temporary building in the grounds where running a cable would be impractical or unnecessarily expensive. Wireless net-working offers a solution to these sorts of problems and although a wireless network is not as inherently secure as its wired coun-terpart, there are some straightforward methods of improving your security. These are examined later in the chapter.

It is still unusual for a workplace network to be entirely wire-less, though it is of course feasible. More usually, there is a wired Ethernet LAN of the type we looked at earlier, with some means of attaching wireless connections to it. Typically, this is done through a Wireless Access Point – which we shall consider shortly. We will begin with the simplest possible wireless network con-sisting of two wireless enabled PCs in an ad hoc network.

Wireless network adaptors

Wireless network adaptors (or cards) are much the same as their wired counterparts except that they have an antenna instead of a connector for an RJ45. Physical installation of these cards is much the same as with the wired ones. More often than not, you need to install software drivers from the manufacturer's CD be-fore fitting the adaptor. Read the instructions that come with it and perhaps look back to Chapter 1, then have a go. If you get it wrong you won't damage anything – just uninstall and start again.

Wireless networking standards

There are a number of wireless networking standards, but only three of these are likely to be of interest to the small business user. These are the 802.11b, 802.11g and 802.11n standards. The 11b standard is the oldest (and slowest) of these so you should, if possible, avoid buying kit which only meets this stand-ard. The 11g standard is faster, and it is backward compatible with the older standard so you can mix equipment on the same network. The latest standard – 11n – is even faster than 11g and is also backward compatible. Whatever you decide to buy, check your existing equipment and make sure that your new kit really *is* backward compatible with it, as some users report that there are still some compatibility issues.

4.2 Ad hoc wireless networks

The simplest wireless network is known as an ad hoc network because it has no formal structure. You can set up a complete network on an ad hoc basis, but this is unusual. For the most part, a complete network is set up using a Wireless Access Point (WAP) and the ad hoc set up is used for occasional connections. A typical use might be a company where staff who work mainly in the field return to the office and need a temporary connection between their laptop/notebook system and the office file store, mail system or Internet connection.

Setting up an ad hoc connection

The easiest way of understanding this is to do it. In this example, we will create a new wireless network on a desktop machine and then configure a laptop machine to connect to it on an ad hoc basis. If necessary, fit a wireless network adaptor to the desktop PC and ensure that the laptop machine has a wireless network adaptor – most modern laptops have one built in.

On the desktop PC:

1 Open the **Control Panel** and select **Wireless Network Setup**.

2 Choose the **Set up a new wireless network** option.

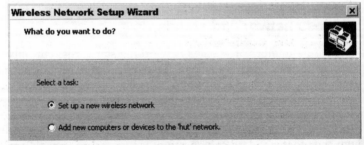

Figure 4.01

3 Click on **Next**.

4 Enter a name for your new network name. This is known as the *Service Set Identifier* (SSID) and in this example it has been set to *haven-wifi*.

5 Click on **Next**.

6 You will now be prompted to choose between USB and manual set up. Choose manual set up as in Figure 4.02.

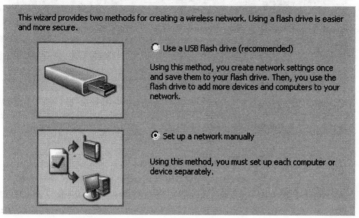

This wizard provides two methods for creating a wireless network. Using a flash drive is easier and more secure.

○ Use a USB flash drive (recommended)

Using this method, you create network settings once and save them to your flash drive. Then, you use the flash drive to add more devices and computers to your network.

◉ Set up a network manually

Using this method, you must set up each computer or device separately.

Figure 4.02

7 Click on **Next**.

8 Click on the button to **Print Network Settings** – you will need these later to set up the other end of your network connection.

9 Click on **Finish** to finish.

Repeat steps 1–9 on the laptop (or second desktop) PC.

Making the connection

With your new wireless adaptor in place, Windows will probably place an icon in the Notification Area (sometimes known as the System Tray) on the right-hand side of the Task Bar at the bottom of the screen. If it does not, there will be an entry in the **Connect To** section of the Start menu or, failing *that*, you can navigate to the **Network Connections** applet in the **Control Panel**.

Click on the icon for your newly installed connection and you will be presented with choices along the lines of those shown in Figure 4.03.

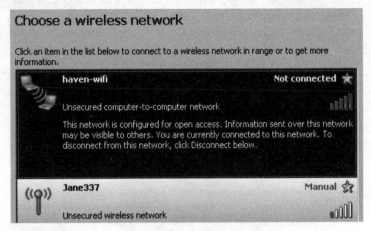

Choose a wireless network

Click an item in the list below to connect to a wireless network in range or to get more information.

haven-wifi — Not connected ⭐

Unsecured computer-to-computer network

This network is configured for open access. Information sent over this network may be visible to others. You are currently connected to this network. To disconnect from this network, click Disconnect below.

Jane337 — Manual ⭐

Unsecured wireless network

Figure 4.03

In this case, there is a choice of the ad hoc connection which you have just created and an unsecured wireless network *Jane337*. This is someone else's network – possibly a neighbour who has not bothered with securing it. Not only would it be unneighbourly to connect to this, it would be a breach of the law. To make sure that you are not offering free network access to the neighbours – or even a business competitor sitting in the car park with a WiFi enabled laptop – see the *Wireless security* section later in this chapter.

4.3 Wireless Access Points

A Wireless Access Point (WAP) – sometimes known as a *base station* – is the wireless equivalent of a hub or switch on a wired network. Except on an entirely wireless network it is attached to a conventional wired network in order to provide a connection for wireless enabled systems. Although it is beyond the scope of this book, which deals only with PCs running Windows, a WAP will enable you to connect any computer such as a Mac or a PC running a different operating system, so long as it supports wireless networking, and the encryption type you have chosen.

Setting up your WAP

Your WAP will have at least one – probably more – Ethernet
ports for connection to a wired LAN. Obviously you will need
to read and follow any installation instructions from the manufacturer, but the general procedure is to attach a PC to the LAN
port of the WAP and do any necessary configuration tasks.

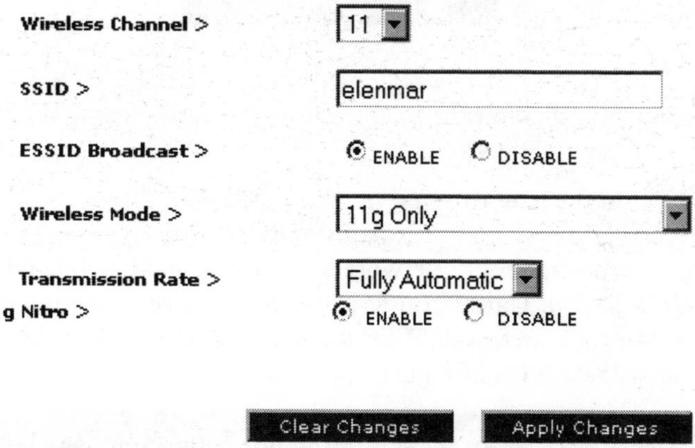

Wireless Channel >	11 ▾
SSID >	elenmar
ESSID Broadcast >	◉ ENABLE ○ DISABLE
Wireless Mode >	11g Only ▾
Transmission Rate >	Fully Automatic ▾
g Nitro >	◉ ENABLE ○ DISABLE

Clear Changes   Apply Changes

Figure 4.04

The **Wireless Channel** is probably best left at the manufacturer's
default setting unless there are definite reasons to do otherwise.

The **SSID** field is the **Service Set Identifier** – this is essentially the
name of your wireless network. Set it to whatever you want – it
is the name which other PCs will 'see' and use to connect to
your wireless network. Note that the SSID is only a *name* for
your network – it does not set up any type of network security.

The **Extended SSID** (ESSID) **Broadcast** field shown here is set to
Enable. This means your access point broadcasts its identity,
making it easy to detect and connect from one of your PCs. This
function can be disabled if you wish – more on security later.

The **Wireless mode** field here is set for '11g only' because the
network in this instance uses only 11g rated equipment. If it
comprised entirely 11b equipment, there is a setting for this.
There is also a setting for a mixed 11b and 11g network. Other,
later, standards are similarly catered for.

The final field – **Transmission Rate** – is probably best left to its
default setting of **Fully Automatic.**

Connecting to your WAP

In order to connect to your WAP from a wireless enabled PC, navigate to **Control Panel > Network Connections** and select the wireless connection icon.

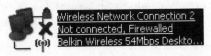

Figure 4.05

Alternatively, click on the icon in the Notification area. Whichever route you choose:

1 Click on the icon to connect. The system will display a list of available networks – probably only one (though you may pick up a neighbour's network as well – see section 4.4, *Wireless security*). Unless you have set up some security on your network already, your WAP will be broadcasting its identity and will state (as in Figure 4.06) that it is insecure.

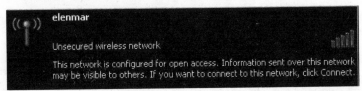

Figure 4.06

2 Click **Connect** now and you will see this security warning.

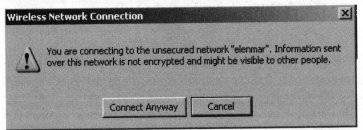

Figure 4.07

3 Click **Connect Anyway** to connect to your network as a test. Bear in mind, that anyone in wireless range can do the same thing until you have put some security measures in place.

4.4 Wireless security

The simplest form of security for the wireless network is to change the SSID field (see Figure 4.04 above) to give it a difficult-to-guess name. Choose one as you would a password – something that's easy for you to remember but difficult for others to guess.

With the new SSID name in place, disable the ESSID function. This means that your network will have a name known only to you which is not broadcast. As it is not broadcast, it will not appear as an available wireless network to anyone else, but as you know that it exists and you know its name you can connect to it. However, if you have items such as media (streaming) players this may not be the case. Even if they are given the settings they may not be able to connect while the network is hidden.

In this example, the name of the wireless network (its SSID) has been changed to Fr1day-99 and the ESSID broadcast function has been disabled. Clicking on the connection icon (**Control Panel > Network Connections > Wireless Network Icon**) indicates 'No wireless networks are in range') – this is what you want.

To connect to your Fr1day-99 network all you need to do is to right-click on the icon and select **Properties** from the context menu. Choose the **Wireless Networks** tab. Ignore the **View Wireless Networks** button – you have taken steps to ensure that your new network won't be listed here. Instead, click the **Add** button – this will open the dialog box shown in Figure 4.08.

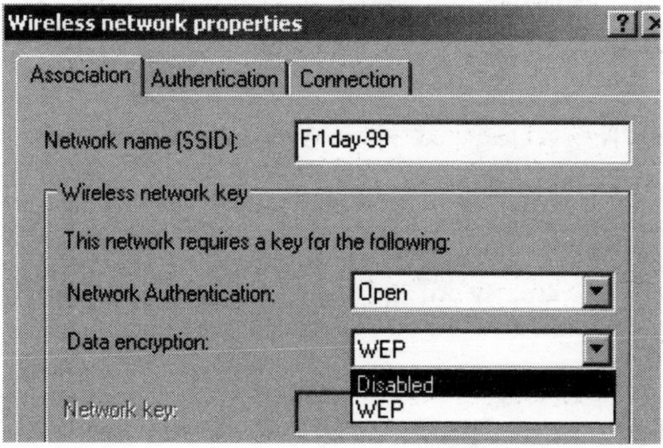

Figure 4.08

Type the SSID into the box, change the **Data encryption** field from *WEP* to *Disabled* and save your changes by clicking **OK**. The new name will appear in the list of available networks, though it is still not connected. Click **OK** to close the dialog box.

Return to your wireless network icon and click on it to connect to your unadvertised network. Now that you have set up the connection manually, the network will show up on your system and can be configured so that you will connect automatically when the PC (or laptop) is in range. However, to anyone else within range your wireless network is invisible.

For most users, the security steps outlined here are probably sufficient. All you really want is to prevent casual or even accidental connections by neighbours or anyone else who happens to come in range. However, there are some more advanced security features which you may like to look at.

Wireless protected access with pre-shared key (WPA-PSK)

This is a means of setting a password on a wireless connection. At the Access Point end of things, choose the WPA-PSK option and choose a password – a pre-shared key. Note the associated data encryption method – in this case it is TKIP.

WPA >	WPA-PSK (no server)
Encryption technique	**TKIP**
Pre-shared Key (PSK)	●●●●●●●●●●

Figure 4.09

1   At the PC end of the connection, navigate to the wireless network connection icon. Right-click and select **Properties**. Choose the **Wireless Networks** tab and select **Properties**. Enter the PSK password and make sure that the data encryption method matches that of your WAP (see Figure 4.10).

2   Click **OK** to save your changes.

3   Return to your network icon and click on it to connect to your unadvertised and now secure network.

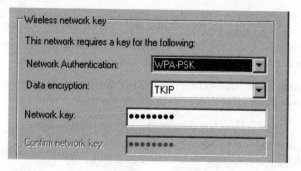

Figure 4.10

Wired Equivalent Privacy (WEP)

Although the security methods we have looked at make it difficult for anyone to gain unauthorized access to your network,
the data is transmitted between PCs in unencrypted form. Anyone with sufficient know-how to access your network (not easy,
but possible) could read that data. As a further level of security
you can encrypt your data so that it can only be decrypted by
someone who has the necessary encryption key. The most widely
used form of encryption for wireless networks is *Wired Equivalent Privacy* (WEP). To set up WEP, you need to access your
WAP setup utility, enable WEP and define an encryption key – a
word or phrase from which a numeric key will be generated.

Clicking **Generate** creates the hexadecimal pairs based on the
passphrase. This becomes, in effect, a password for the network.

WEP is the basic mechanism to transmit your data securely over the wireless network. Matching
encryption keys must be setup on your device g and wireless client devices to use WEP.

Security Mode:	64-bit WEP				
⦿ Key 1:	D7	14	91	68	2D
○ Key 2:	75	85	8C	07	52
○ Key 3:	EA	AB	FD	B7	2B
○ Key 4:	D8	E8	E4	18	F0
Note :	To automatically generate hex pairs using a PassPhrase, input it here.				
Passphrase >	mypassphrase	Generate			

Clear Changes   Apply Changes

Figure 4.11 Generating a WEP encryption key.

To connect and read the data sent across your network it has to be known and implemented at both ends of the connection. Once you have entered the WEP settings on the WAP, you need to configure the connection through Windows.

1 Navigate to your existing wireless connection, right-click and select **Properties** from the context menu.

2 Choose the **Wireless Networks** tab and click **Add**.

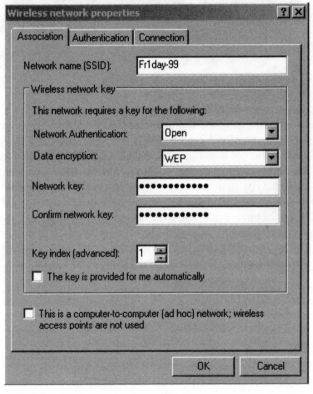

Figure 4.12

3 The passphrase from Figure 4.11 is entered as the Network key – this is not displayed as you type, for security reasons.

4 Save your changes by clicking **OK**.

Connecting to a secure wireless network with Vista

This is a very similar process to connecting in XP.

1 Use **Start > Network** and choose the **Connect to a Network** option. Vista will show a list of available networks – in this case the Secure Wireless network that we set up earlier in the chapter – Fr1day-99.

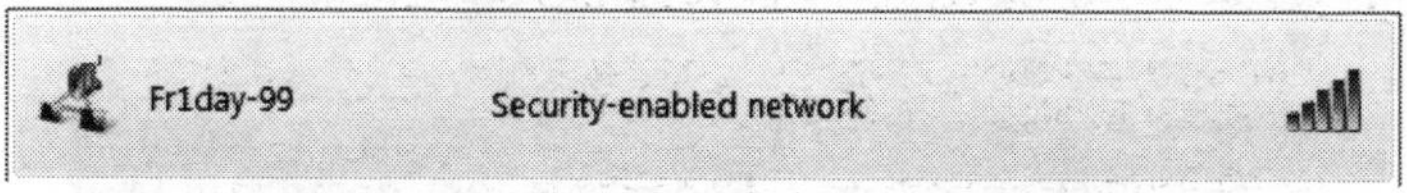

Fr1day-99   Security-enabled network

Figure 4.13

2 Highlight the entry in the list and click **Connect**. You will be prompted for the security key.

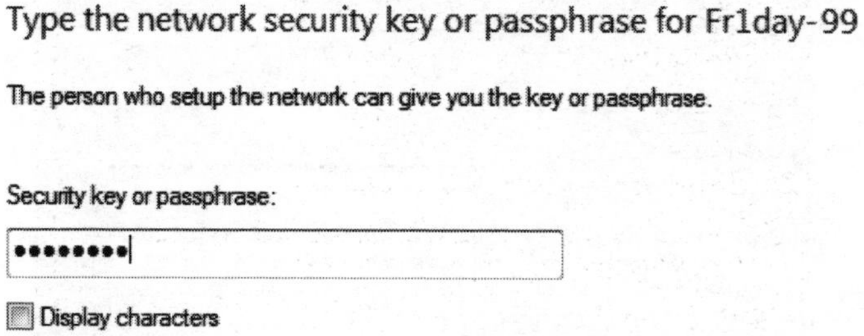

Type the network security key or passphrase for Fr1day-99

The person who setup the network can give you the key or passphrase.

Security key or passphrase:

••••••••|

☐ Display characters

Figure 4.14

If you have provided the correct key, Vista will now connect to your chosen network.

3 Type it in and click on **Next**.

Connected to Fr1day-99 - getting IP address...

Figure 4.15

Job done.

Summary

This chapter has examined the basics of wireless networking. We have looked at the simplest of networks – the ad hoc connection which is especially suitable for temporary links between laptops or a laptop and a desktop PC.

We have looked at more structured wireless LANs using a Wireless Access Point (WAP).

We have also considered the basics of security as they apply to small wireless networks. Security is considered at greater length in Chapter 14.

05 planning your network

In this chapter you will learn:

- how to evaluate services to users
- how to plan for growth
- how to determine the best physical infrastructure
- how to plan for low maintenance costs
- how to estimate installation costs

5.1 Starting the plan

A common problem with small business networks is that the network 'just grew'. It is all too easy to cobble something together to meet the needs of the moment and to neglect the needs of longer-term operation, security and management. Planning and monitoring progress and performance are the key to avoiding the worst pitfalls.

In a very small business it may be possible simply to have one or more round table discussions in which you (or someone) takes notes. Where more people are involved you made need to have a series of discussions or even individual interviews. Whatever approach you take to the top-level planning process, you need to be clear about what you are doing and to document everything at each stage. You need to assess and record what you, as an organization, are currently doing, what will be required immediately of the network and its scope for future development.

Apart from the purely technical aspects, discussion and consultation can be good for morale. If your colleagues feel that they are being considered, that the network will bring them benefits in terms of easier working, you will find it easier to implement your chosen solution.

5.2 Services to users

A good starting point for planning is to consider what equipment is currently providing services to users. Most businesses have several PCs and one or more printers. They probably have an Internet connection. Start by listing the existing equipment and services, then consider how to incorporate these into the network, and what additional services you want to provide.

Printing

One of the driving forces behind early networks was the ability to share printers. If you intend to provide print services on your network you should consider whether a printer (or two) can be attached to a workstation and simply shared through Windows or whether to use some form of dedicated server. Your choice here will depend largely on the volume of print jobs that you process in a normal working day. For light usage, a Windows share on one of your workstations will probably be sufficient. On the other hand, if anyone does a lot of printing, then the workstation that acts as a print server will slow to a crawl at busy times. In theses circumstances you need to consider a dedicated print server and/or print access boxes.

File services

We looked at the benefits of sharing files and using a shared file store in Chapter 1, *Getting started*. The advantages of a shared file store, even on our two-PC network in the first chapters, are fairly obvious: security of data, ease of backups, etc. If you want to extend this service to your larger network, you will need to consider using a PC simply as a file server (even on a peer network). You need to consider the size and power of the PC to be used for this purpose, a secure location for it and the backup strategy needed to preserve your data.

Internet access

Access to the Internet is as much a part of most businesses these days as access to the telephone. If you are planning on giving everyone access to the Internet you need to consider how to handle both access and security. As with the print server example, a small number of users can receive Internet services through a PC doubling up as a workstation and a gateway to the Net. However, if you have more than a very few users requiring Internet access, a more effective and secure solution is to use a dedicated gateway PC as your router/firewall or to buy a dedicated hardware router. There are a number of combined ADSL modem/routers aimed mainly at the small office/home office user which may meet your needs.

E-mail

E-mail is now fundamental to the way we do business, so the choice for most of us is not so much *if* we provide e-mail services as *how* we go about it. It is possible to run your own mail servers for both incoming and outgoing mail, but the administrative overheads are high and there are security considerations. Like your website (below) there is a case to be made for external hosting of your e-mail services.

Website

Even small companies these days have a website. Even if you don't want to sell products directly over the Net it is useful to have a web presence if only as a shop window where you can promote the organization, give contact details, details of services and events, and so on. Running your own web server is possible, of course, but as soon as you start serving pages out on to the Web you will incur administrative overheads and more complex security arrangements. A simpler solution for most small organizations is to buy a hosted package from a specialist firm. Typically these packages consist of a registered domain name – *www.yourcompanyname.com* – with several e-mail addresses in the form *whoever@yourcompanyname.com*. If the package doesn't include SMTP service (the Simple Mail Transfer Protocol, for sending e-mail) then you can buy a subscription for this from a specialist provider at very little cost.

Chapter 9, *Internet and e-mail* looks at these topics in more detail.

5.3 Planning for growth

If you have worked through the material so far, you should by now have a fairly clear idea about the current state of the equipment and services. You may also have learnt where the various pinch points and bottlenecks in your system are. The next stage is to decide, through consultation with users and managers, how best to meet their needs now and in the future.

A useful next step is to summarize the findings in a draft report and discuss this with a senior manager (if you are working in a traditional hierarchy) or with those concerned (in a small co-operative enterprise). The purpose of this is not to discuss the benefits of networks in general, but to establish your business aims and objectives, and how the network can best serve these objectives. For example, are you planning to expand the range or volume of your business services over the next year (or two, or five)? If so, you need to plan now: how many additional staff? How many additional PCs? How many additional access points?

With the top-level interviews and discussions done and documented, the next stage of the process is to take a look at specific tasks in the organization, how they are carried out and by whom.

How many users?

In many organizations there is one PC per desktop and one worker per desk. The most common software configuration is Windows and the customary office tools: word processor, spreadsheet, etc. A standard software build of this kind – provided that it meets users' needs – has much to recommend it in terms of keeping maintenance tasks simple.

However, not every employee will spend the whole of their working day at a PC. For example, an organization that gives career advice may have PCs which are used for public access to a database using a generic guest account. The staff who are advisers, will spend much of their time interacting with the public, but will need network access from time to time to update records, retrieve information or do ad hoc Internet research.

In terms of capacity – storage, backup media, even the Internet connection speed – the number of users is a more important consideration than the number of PCs. Where you intend to use a shared file store – whether on a peer or client/server network – the number of user accounts (one for each member of staff plus any guest accounts) will be greater than the number of PCs.

How many PCs?

If you haven't already done so, walk around and count them. Make a note of where they are and who uses them. Make a note, too, of their capacity: size of hard disk, RAM and whether they already have a network connector suitable for your proposed network. It may be useful to assign each PC a number and mark it with a sticky label.

At the end of this exercise you will have a list of PCs, each of which can be categorized under one of three headings: 'network ready', 'upgradeable' or 'ready for the skip'. This information feeds directly into your (later) cost estimates.

5.4 Which jobs are done where?

Many jobs in a typical office are done by one person, using a single PC on their own desk. All that is required for these machines is that they can connect to the network to access network services. For most office applications, all that is required is basic hardware (there is no need for high end graphics or sound cards), a professional version of Windows – XP or Vista – and the usual productivity tools: word processor, spreadsheet, etc.

Some organizations may have specialized PCs – for example, 3D design software usually requires a high hardware specification: as much RAM as you can afford and a quality graphics card that can cost as much as an entire budget system. Add to this specialist input devices such as graphics tablets or specialist output devices such as plotters and you are looking at a substantial investment. From the point of view of physical security alone, this equipment needs to be well away from any part of the premises to which the public have access. From the point of view of maintenance this is a special build – not only are its software components different, but you may need to carry additional spares such as a Power Supply Unit (PSU) or even a spare graphics card to maintain its availability. See Chapter 7, *Fault tolerance and disaster recovery* for more on this.

At the other end of the scale is the general purpose, multi-user PC. From a maintenance perspective, this would use the common workhorse build of hardware and software that you use for your other general-purpose office PCs. If you are going to use a peer network (more later), then each of these shared PCs will need a separate account for each user – which can make system administration complex if there are more than a handful of users – or you can use a guest account whose password is known to all staff that use the system. The shared password or guest user solution is an obvious security risk.

Finally, there may be machines which don't need to be attached to the network. An organization which offers careers advice to students or the public may simply run CD-based specialist software packages and print the results. A simple solution would, perhaps, be a standalone machine with its own local printer where people can be allowed minimally supervised use of the standalone system without the need to consider network security.

5.5 Capacity planning

At this stage of the planning process you should have a fairly clear idea of what is required to meet users' present needs and what may be required to improve services to them. You will be able to specify additional equipment requirements and provide rough cost estimates and, if you have to sell the idea to management, it will pay to have an estimate of the expected benefits in terms of work flow and improved efficiency.

In the course of your consultations with users, you may have identified problem areas where extra capacity would be beneficial. For example, if people regularly have to stand in line to wait for a printout, an additional printer may be cost-effective.

A further dimension of your plan will involve some level of planning for future needs. The rate of technological change is such that we can all expect year-on-year increases in what we need just to get the job done. In addition, planned expansion or diversification of business activities will mean additional staff, which in turn means extra capacity. Your plan should take into account future needs. You need to consider where you are going to be in 2, 5 or even 10 years.

Cable installations generally outlive other network components by several generations of upgrades and they can be expensive and troublesome to upgrade in a piecemeal fashion. In terms of both quality and number of connections the rule for cabling is simple – over-specify.

File servers, including the shared file store machine on a peer network need as much RAM and the fastest, biggest and most reliable disk subsystem that you can afford. Like cable installations, centralized storage should be specified to outlive other network components. Replacing a single PC or a printer on your network may inconvenience one or two staff for an hour or two. A major server upgrade will inconvenience everyone as well as having implications for data integrity and security. Specifying server hardware is a topic in Chapter 12, *Client/server networks*.

5.6 Physical infrastructure

The best possible physical infrastructure for your network will be the one that uses the least hardware and cabling needed to do the job. In addition, it should be secure and simple to maintain and extend. The key decisions at this stage are the location of the server room and the number and location of access points.

The server room

One of the most fundamental decisions that you will have to make is the location of your server room. Even if you are not using a dedicated server box as such, there will be some central point where cables attach to your main (probably only) patch panel, switch or router. This is variously designated as a 'server room', 'communications closet' or 'central cabling nexus' – the terminology is less important than the selection criteria for this key location.

The server room should, above all, be secure. Provided that it is big enough and sufficiently well ventilated, the cupboard under the stairs may prove to be ideal. Alternatively, you may locate everything in any space that can be physically secured. As you will see in Chapter 14, *Security*, network security as a whole begins with the physical security of the hardware.

Another important consideration is the length and complexity of the cable runs. Category 5/6 cable has a maximum length of 100 metres (328 feet) from end to end, so your server room should, ideally, be within this distance of all your intended connection points. There are ways around this limitation, of course. You can deploy extra switches or repeaters where necessary, but this adds to both the complexity and cost of your network and should be avoided if possible. Chapter 6, *Expanding your network* considers the deployment of network hardware in more detail.

Connection points

Providing your patch panel, switch or hub can offer sufficient connections at the server room end you can't have too many connection points around your offices. Every PC that you connect, now or in the future, will need a wall socket to connect to the network. If you are going to use 'true' network printers – that have an RJ45 port built into them – or printers that attach through an access box that has its own IP address, then each of these will require its own wall socket.

Another possible use for spare connection points is to enable staff (or guests) with laptop/notebook systems to make a temporary connection to your network to exchange files, access the

Internet or to print. The cost of providing a few extr~~
tion points when you first cable your premises is ne~~
comparison with the cost of putting in an additional c~~
later.

Wireless access

Even if you don't want to deploy wireless connections for the
main body of your network, you may want to consider one or
two wireless connections if you have any difficult-to-reach locations or temporary offices in portable buildings. Although it adds
slightly to initial costs and introduces some additional security
considerations (see Chapter 4, *Wireless networks*), wireless may
be a way of dealing with awkward connections, leaving you free
to concentrate your effort on the main cable runs.

5.7 Peer network or client/server

The decision over which network type is best for your business
is discussed in Chapter 12, *Client/server networks*. It is quite
possible that you will start with a peer network, outgrow it in a
couple of years and then decide to go for a client/server system.
The decision need not be made now, but a robust, well-planned
infrastructure with plenty of connection points and a properly
secured server room will help to future proof your installation
ahead of such an upgrade.

5.8 Building ease of maintenance into the specification

Once your network is up and running, it will need to be main-
tained. You may need to provide additional services for users,
additional applications may need to be installed and operating
systems reinstalled from time to time. Chapter 11, *Building a
node* looks at some important aspects of maintaining your network. However, what is ideal from the maintenance point of
view may not suit everyone else in the organization. There are
essentially three competing interests: those of the initial purchaser
of the equipment, those of the end user and those of the maintenance staff.

In networking, as in many areas of business life, beware of the false economy. It may be tempting, particularly in a small enterprise or a not-for-profit operation, to buy this week's special offer from a local or online retailer and these can, of course, offer value for money. The problem with this approach is that you may well end up with different hardware specifications and even different operating system versions on all your PCs.

Regardless of the merits of each PC considered individually, maintaining your network becomes more complex – and therefore more costly – with each variation that you introduce.

The end user

From the user's point of view the best possible PC is one that is tailored to his or her individual needs, and some machines – those that are used for specialist applications – may require a hardware and software build that is specific to that machine, that user and those tasks. Providing there is a business case for this – fine. The network and the PCs exist to meet the needs of the users and the business objectives of the enterprise. However, every customization of a PC adds complexity to the network *as a system* which, in turn, adds to administrative and maintenance costs.

Maintenance staff

The ideal setup from a maintenance point of view would consist of identical PCs – same hardware, same operating system version, same applications. Standardization makes it possible to deploy a limited number of images or build scripts to streamline maintenance tasks and reduce costs.

5.9 Installation costs

The planning process is not a simple linear one. You will begin by planning your network installation from a technical point of view – number of PCs needed, length of cable runs, etc. Depending on the size of the undertaking and the degree of formality that you prefer, you will prepare something between a simple shopping list and a materials schedule. Either way, you will end up with a list of hardware – and possibly additional software – requirements needed to implement your initial design ideas.

All of the equipment which you are going to need is readily available from High Street and online retailers, so price comparisons are easy. Once you have some cost estimates, you can review your original plan, revising as necessary to trim any unnecessary expenditure. This may also be a good time to consider alternatives. For example, changing your mind now about whether to connect a particular office by wireless rather than by a difficult cable run will be cheaper and easier than changing your mind after you have made firm purchasing decisions or placed contracts.

In order to estimate costs, it may be useful to divide the job into contractable chunks. Consider what aspects can be done in-house and those which can be contracted. For premises cabling in particular, it may be worth getting a quote from a specialist contractor. Similarly, for the supply of PCs you may like to get a quote from a local supplier or contractor for your basic workstation hardware and operating systems.

The object of the exercise is to end up with the best possible network which will meet your present and future operational needs at a cost that you can afford.

Summary

In this chapter we have considered the process of planning your network in terms of meeting current and future business needs. We have mapped these business needs on to possible combinations of hardware, cabling and connectors and seen how to estimate the costs involved. The process of planning is threefold:

Consultation – the purpose of a network is to meet the users' needs. Time spent talking to people to establish what these needs are is time well spent. Apart from technical information, a sense of involvement by the users can make everyone's life a lot easier.

cont...

Documentation – whatever you do, write it down. You will interview staff, you will get quotes from suppliers, and you will obtain information from the Internet. All of this needs to be recorded. You will need to sketch out possible cable runs and decide the locations of network devices from printers to hubs and switches. Write it down.

Iteration – planning a network is not a simple linear process. Establish top-level goals. Document them. Discuss them with staff and management. Estimate costs. Revise and refine your goals. Document them. Discuss them with staff and management.

Time and effort spent on the planning process now will produce a better, more effective network for years to come. It will also produce the documentation necessary to maintain your network.

06

**expanding
your network**

In this chapter you will learn:

- about network addresses and
  addressing methods

- about the role of hubs, switches
  and routers

- about user accounts and
  patterns of work and use

6.1 Network addressing schemes

As we have seen in previous chapters, each PC on your network needs its own IP address in much the same way as each phone needs its own number. Other devices, such as network-enabled printers, also need their own IP addresses.

Private networks (as opposed to public networks such as the Internet) use a reserved set of private IP addresses. Small private networks generally use a Class 'C' address range. The class 'C' address range supports up to 254 connected devices – PC work-stations, servers, network printers and so on – so this is more than enough for most small businesses.

From a practical point of view, all that is required is that you choose an appropriate class 'C' range and stick with it. Your class 'C' address will have the form 192.168.xxx.yyy. You choose a value in the range 0–255 for the xxx field and this, with the previous two fields becomes the 'network part' of the address. In the example which follows we will use the value '2' in this field. This means that the address of any PC on your network will be 192.168.2.yyy. The 192.168.2 is the network part of the address – the equivalent of the exchange code for a phone system – and the yyy part will be a number in the range 1–254 which you will assign to each machine. This is known as the 'host part' of the address. Like a phone number, this has to be unique for each attached PC. A typical IP address – 192.168.2.23 – for our network example looks like this:

Network part (exchange code)   **Host part (phone number)**
         192.168.2.   23

Within our LAN, the network part of the address must be the same for every attached device and the host part must be different for each device.

Subnet masks

Network classes are distinguished by subnet masks. When you are setting up a Windows PC it usually reads the IP address that you enter and calculates the appropriate subnet mask and fills it in for you. For the record, the standard subnet masks are:

> Class A – 255.000.000.000
>
> Class B – 255.255.000.000
>
> Class C – 255.255.255.000

Having decided on an addressing scheme, we have now to apply it to all the machines on our network. There are three methods of doing this: static addressing, the Dynamic Host Configuration Protocol (DHCP) and Automatic Private IP Addressing (APIPA). We will look at each of them in turn.

Static IP addresses

On a small network – say 10 PCs in the same building – it is possible to adopt a static IP addressing scheme. To do this, you will need to choose a network address for the network as a whole and then enter an IP address (and other details) on each workstation, taking care that there are no duplicate addresses. If it helps, think of this as equivalent to allocating phone numbers on a single exchange: the exchange number being the network part of the address 192.168.2 and the individual phone number being the last field – a value in the range 1 to 254.

Windows – XP and Vista – uses a dialog box for entering the IP address information and will fill in the subnet mask for you.

In Vista:

1 Navigate to **Control Panel > Network Center**.

2 Click **Manage Network Connections** in the menu on the left.

3 Right-click on the LAN adaptor icon and select **Properties**.

4 Select the entry for **Internet Protocol Version 4 (TCP IPv4)**.

5 Click **Properties** and you will see something like Figure 6.01. This shows the default setting for Windows PCs, which is to obtain an IP address automatically.

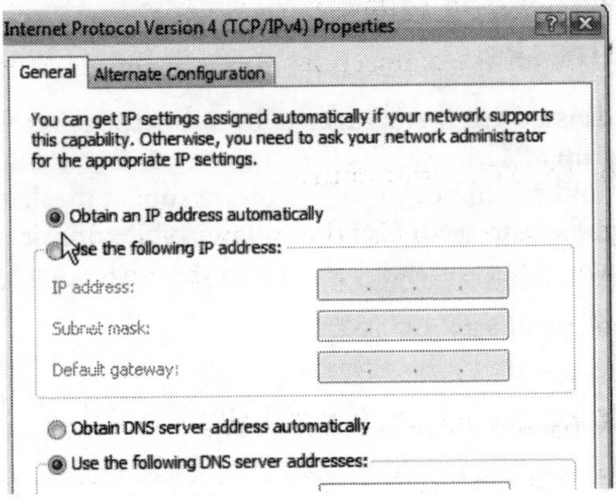

Figure 6.01

6 To change the Windows default, select **Use the following IP address** and enter the values as shown in Figure 6.02, or whatever values you have chosen for your network.

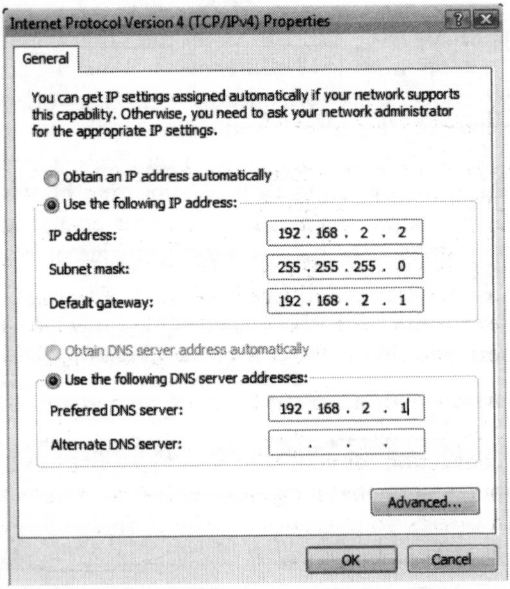

Figure 6.02

7 When you have finished, click **OK** to save your changes.

In XP:

1 Navigate to **Control Panel > Network Settings**.

2 Right-click on the connection icon and choose **Properties**.

3 Scroll down the list and highlight the **Internet Protocol** entry.

4 Click on the **Properties** button.

5 Change the setting to **Use the following IP address** and enter your own values or those shown in the Vista example.

6 Save your changes.

The gateway and preferred DNS entries

These fields contain the IP addresses that are needed for your PC to connect to the Internet. The first of them is the address of the gateway PC or router which connects directly to the Internet, and the second one tells the PC where to look up the IP addresses of Internet sites through the Domain Name Service. If your Internet Service Provider (ISP) has given you an IP address for the preferred DNS server, use that. Otherwise use the same address as the gateway box.

How the gateway works

When you connect with another device on your LAN, the system recognizes that the target machine is on the same network – in this case the network defined by 192.168.2. If the target address is in a different range, then the system will assume that you require a device on a different network. Since it can't route your request within the LAN, it needs to know what to do with your request, and that is the role of the default gateway.

When provided with an IP address (or a computer name that resolves to an IP address) on the same network, the system will make the connection for you. When provided with an IP address (or a computer name that it cannot resolve to a local IP address) the system directs your request to the default gateway which attempts to route your request to an external network.

How DNS works

The Domain Name System extends this principle to finding Internet IP addresses. If you type the name of a website – www.example.com – into a browser Address bar, this makes no sense to your LAN. It cannot resolve the text address to a local IP address so it passes it to the default gateway which in turn passes the address to a DNS server somewhere out there. Usually the IP address of the DNS server is allocated dynamically by your ISP, so all you need to supply is the address of the gateway machine which will then obtain this information for you. If this is not the case, then put the ISP provided address for the DNS server in the appropriate field. Either way, what happens, is this:

♦ You, the user, request a connection to a device that is not on your LAN.

♦ The LAN passes the unknown address to the gateway.

♦ The gateway machine sends the name of the requested connection to a Domain Name Server.

♦ The Domain Name Server resolves the request to a numeric IP address and passes it back to your LAN (or returns an error message if the address cannot be resolved).

Choosing the gateway machine's IP address

Obviously, it is of critical importance that the IP address of the gateway machine uses the same addressing system as the rest of the network, so it is common practice to give it a static IP address at the bottom of the range that you defined for your LAN. Even where you use other methods of allocating IP addresses on the rest of your network, the gateway address is static. In the example that we have used here, the gateway has been give the address 192.168.2.1 – the bottom of the chosen range. Even if we use other – dynamic – addressing schemes for the remainder of the LAN, the gateway machine will have a static IP address, as will any other server machine or network printer.

The advantages of static IP addresses

For a very small network – say 10 machines in the same building – static IP addressing has some advantages. It is very easy to set up – decide which machine is going to have which IP address – and allocate addresses according to your chosen scheme. Since you have to allocate static addresses to some machines such as the gateway box why not use static IPs for all of them?

The disadvantages of static IP addresses

There are two reasons why you may not want to use static IP addresses for all of your LAN – complexity and flexibility. As the network grows in size, you will have more static IP addresses to keep track of and if you are not careful this can become time-consuming. In addition, each time you add a PC or other device to the network you will have to allocate it a unique IP address and keep track of that too. If you want to add and remove PCs to your network on a temporary basis – say a laptop that a user has brought from home – it will have to be allocated its own unique static IP address. This too, can be time-consuming.

For these reasons, complexity and flexibility, larger networks use dynamic methods of allocating IP addresses for most of their PCs. The most important and widely used of these methods is the Dynamic Host Configuration Protocol (DHCP) which was developed by Microsoft to meet the needs of large – sometimes very large – networks.

Dynamic Host Configuration Protocol (DHCP)

Each node or *host* on a network needs the same basic information to function as part of the network: a unique IP address in the correct range, an appropriate subnet mask and the addresses of the default gateway and DNS servers. We have seen how this can be achieved through allocating the necessary values to each machine on the network in the form of static IPs. DHCP provides the means of automating the process through the use of a DHCP server to dole them out as and when required.

A DHCP server is a piece of software running on a machine somewhere on your network. It may be on a PC which you have configured for this purpose (Linux-based systems such as Mitel's *SME server* or Point Clark Network's *Clark Connect* both provide DHCP services amongst others) or it may be incorporated into another network device such as one of the multi-purpose ADSL modem/routers that are sold for home and business use.

Whatever device you use to provide DHCP services for your network, you will need to provide information on the IP addresses, the subnet mask, default gateway and DNS servers for the network as a whole. This information is then passed automatically to each PC on the network for which it has been configured, to obtain an IP address automatically – the default value for Windows PCs. You will also have to provide a range of values for the DHCP pool from which addresses are selected. Figure 6.03 shows an interface for configuring a hardware-based combined gateway and DHCP server on a small network.

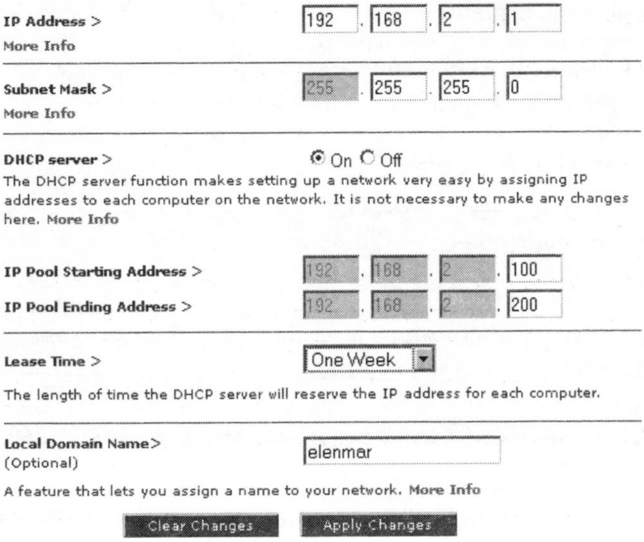

IP Address >
More Info

192 . 168 . 2 . 1

Subnet Mask >
More Info

255 . 255 . 255 . 0

DHCP server >   ⊙ On ○ Off
The DHCP server function makes setting up a network very easy by assigning IP addresses to each computer on the network. It is not necessary to make any changes here. More Info

IP Pool Starting Address >   192 . 168 . 2 . 100

IP Pool Ending Address >   192 . 168 . 2 . 200

Lease Time >   One Week ▼

The length of time the DHCP server will reserve the IP address for each computer.

Local Domain Name>
(Optional)

elenmar

A feature that lets you assign a name to your network. More Info

Clear Changes   Apply Changes

Figure 6.03

The first two fields show the (static) IP address of the server itself and the subnet mask appropriate to this – a class 'C' – network. (Note that the IP address of the server is the default gateway address that will be provided to each of the clients on your LAN. The DHCP service itself doesn't require an IP address as it is 'discovered' as part of the DHCP service – see the section *How DHCP works*, below.)

The On/Off radio buttons control whether or not the DHCP service is running – you should only run one DHCP server on your network.

The DHCP pool

The start and end addresses for the DHCP pool indicate the range of IP addresses available for dynamic allocation. In this instance, the pool is defined to make addresses 100–200 available for dynamic allocation, i.e. you can attach 101 PCs to your network and they can all have a unique IP address. The remaining IP addresses are available for anything – such as a server or network printer – that needs a static IP address.

The lease time is the length of time that the client PC keeps the dynamically allocated address before having to renew it – more in the section below.

The final field, local domain name, is the – optional – name that you give to your network.

How DHCP works

When you attach a new PC to your network, unless it has been allocated a static IP address it will, by default, broadcast a query to the network seeking an IP address from a DHCP server. The DHCP server is listening for such requests and will respond by allocating a free IP address from its pool of available addresses – the pool which you defined when setting up your server. The DHCP server will also allocate other values – which you set up earlier – such as subnet mask, default gateway address and DNS server address.

The IP address is not allocated permanently, but on a renewable lease, in much the same way as you may have a lease on a rented house, i.e. you have the right to use it for the duration of the lease and the lease can be renewed by mutual agreement.

In the example shown in Figure 6.03, the lease has been set for one week. During the lifetime of that lease, the client PC can renew it when 50% of the time has expired or, failing that it may be renewed at 87.5% or, failing that, at the end of the lease. This means that if you remove a PC from your network, its IP address will be returned to the pool at the end of the lease time and will be available for use by another PC.

Figure 6.04 shows part of the output of the IPCONFIG /ALL command. It tells us that the network adaptor on the PC is using

```
Physical Address. . . . . . . . . : 00-0C-41-25-C3-7D
Dhcp Enabled. . . . . . . . . . . : Yes
Autoconfiguration Enabled . . . . : Yes
IP Address. . . . . . . . . . . . : 192.168.2.100
Subnet Mask . . . . . . . . . . . : 255.255.255.0
Default Gateway . . . . . . . . . : 192.168.2.1
DHCP Server . . . . . . . . . . . : 192.168.2.1
DNS Servers . . . . . . . . . . . : 192.168.2.1
Lease Obtained. . . . . . . . . . : 12 July 2006 09:44:26
Lease Expires . . . . . . . . . . : 19 July 2006 09:44:26
```

Figure 6.04

DHCP, it shows the allocated IP address – 192.168.2.100 (which is at the bottom of the DHCP pool range that we defined earlier), subnet mask and other addresses. The lease, in this instance, has been set to one week. If the PC is in use during that week its IP address will be renewed automatically. If it is not used for over a week, it will have to obtain a fresh IP address from the DHCP server – again, automatically. If it is removed from the network, then its IP address becomes available for another PC to use after its lease has expired.

6.2 Automatic Private IP Addressing (APIPA)

Automatic Private IP Addressing (APIPA) is a feature of Windows operating systems. As we have seen previously, Windows is set by default to obtain an IP address automatically so, unless you have configured your system to use a static IP address, it will look for a DHCP server. If it doesn't find a DHCP server, Windows defaults to the APIPA system and allocates itself an IP address from a specially reserved range of addresses which are used for this purpose and the (class B) subnet mask of 255.255.0.0. If you go back to Chapter 1 and look at the two-PC network that we created there, you will see an example of APIPA at work. We neither allocated static IP addresses, nor were we running a DHCP server but, in spite of this our two PCs networked themselves. This is sometimes referred to as the zero configuration option and it can be of some use in some very limited circumstances.

When to use APIPA

If you have only a small network – fewer than 25 PCs – and you don't want to connect to the Internet or route any traffic outside your LAN, then APIPA will do the job with the minimum of fuss (zero configuration) though it will be considerably less efficient than a static IP scheme or using DHCP.

A Windows PC which is set to obtain its IP address automatically looks for a DHCP server. If it doesn't find one, then it falls back to APIPA. It will then check, at five-minute intervals, for a DHCP server and will reconfigure itself using DHCP if it can. This means that on a LAN which uses APIPA, every PC will do this at five-minute intervals. This increases the network traffic, time and resources, and impairs overall network performance. For more than a couple of PCs that don't need to access the Internet, APIPA is probably more trouble than it is worth. Its main use, in practice, is as a fall-back system which will give some local networking connectivity in the event of your DHCP server failing.

6.3 Hubs, switches and routers

These are all network devices which create the connections between cables that are the physical basis of your network. Except in the special case of two PCs connected by a crossover cable (as in the example in Chapter 1) you will need some cabling nexus to join it all together. There are three device types available for this purpose: hubs, switches and routers.

Hubs

Hubs – sometimes known as workgroup hubs – are the simplest of these devices. Figure 6.05 shows a typical workgroup hub.

It has a number of ports which allow you to plug in an Ethernet cable using the standard RJ45 connector. It may have a specially designated 'uplink port' so that it can be linked to another hub, though this is not always the case.

A hub works at a very simple level. At its most basic level of functioning it merely receives a signal on one port which it then replicates on all other ports – the electronic equivalent of a megaphone. This means that if one PC on the network wants to communicate with one other, then the signal is sent to all nodes on the network, which merely ignore it if the communication is not

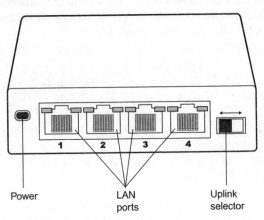

Power   LAN   Uplink
            ports   selector

Figure 6.05 A typical workgroup hub.

intended for them. This is obviously wasteful of resources. Passive hubs of this type have largely been superseded by devices which have some sort of processing power built into them. These may be variously described as 'active' hubs, or 'multi-port repeaters'. For most users, the hub has largely been superseded by various types of Ethernet switch.

Switches

The switch is usually the device of choice for an Ethernet LAN. Like a hub it has a number of ports where you connect your network cables, and at a glance, the physical box may be difficult to distinguish from a hub. However, a switch works in a more sophisticated way because it has some processing power built into it. Whereas a passive hub merely replicates a signal across all its ports and leaves the processing of that signal to the connected PCs (or other devices) a switch builds a 'switching table' based on the physical addresses of the transmitting devices. Thus, if node A wants to communicate with node B, the switch will create a dedicated connection between them. This means that other nodes can communicate with each other simultaneously through other switched connections. If a hub works rather like a megaphone – one person at a time talks and everyone else listens – then a switch works more like a telephone exchange where several one-to-one connections can be made at the same time.

Switches vary in their size, complexity of operation and their price tags. Large, sophisticated switches support features such as virtual LANs and may be deployed as part of large multi-switch networks. This level of processing power and features is probably excessive for the smaller business. However, further down the feature (and price) range there are workgroup switches. These provide the basic operational advantage of switching several one-to-one connections simultaneously without the additional features built into their more sophisticated (and expensive) counterparts.

Routers

Whereas hubs and switches make connections within a LAN, a router is a device which routes signals from one network to another. The commonest example of this is that of a router which you use to connect your LAN to the Internet. Even where you are using a PC that has been configured with Windows Internet Connection Sharing, you are using a router (in this case the connection sharing PC) to connect your LAN – defined by its range of private IP addresses – to the wider world of the Internet with its variety of public IP addresses.

Large corporate networks and the Internet itself use big sophisticated routers, and the big brand name in this field is Cisco Systems. However, for the small business (or even the ambitious home user) there are a number of more manageable (and affordable) routers which you can use to connect your LAN to the Internet. A number of companies – such as Belkin and D-link – make devices which combine switching capabilities for your LAN, the capability to connect your LAN to the Internet (routing) and the means to dial into your Internet Service Provider (ISP) through a built-in ADSL modem. Many of these combination products also incorporate a wireless access point and a hardware firewall, all in the same box. Price tags are typically in double (rather than treble) figures and they generally offer good value for money for the small business user. Figure 6.06 shows a typical combination device of this type.

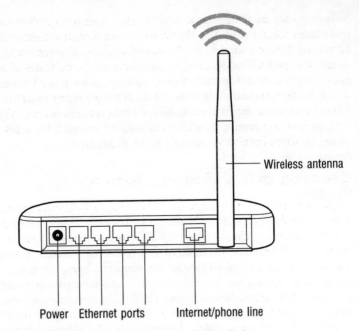

Power   Ethernet ports   Internet/phone line

Figure 6.06 A typical combination router/modem/hub.

6.4 User accounts and patterns of work

Many of the decisions that you make about your network – the equipment you choose, the addressing scheme you use – will depend on how you and your colleagues use the network. The needs of a small group which is mainly office-based will be different from those of a group where (say) salespeople come and go and need occasional ad hoc connections to synchronize files between laptops and the main office system.

User accounts on a peer network

Every user on your network needs a password-protected user account. If, as in many small offices, each person sits at the same PC at the same desk each day, then all they need is a user account on that machine and access to the shared file store.

Where a user uses more than one PC they will need a user account on each of the PCs on the network and access to the shared file store. Where a user regularly uses several PCs – so-called hot desking – they will need a user account on all the machines that they use. The administrative overhead of keeping track of user accounts and passwords for several users across many machines soon becomes a major headache for whoever administers the system and you would be wise to consider moving from a peer network to a client/server system (see Chapter 12).

Choosing an IP addressing scheme

Most workplace LANs these days require an Internet connection, so the APIPA system will be of little use. This leaves a choice between using static IPs or using a DHCP server. Where you have a small number of PCs and few ad hoc connections you can opt for static IP addressing – keeping track of a dozen or so IP addresses on a system which doesn't change frequently is not particularly onerous. When you add a further connection to your network, you will have to assign and manually configure the IP address on the new machine. Providing the IP address is compatible with the rest of your LAN and does not duplicate an existing address, this too is relatively straightforward.

If, on the other hand, you regularly make and break connections for guests or staff who bring in laptops to make temporary connections – wireless or wired – it is far easier to use an automatic system for allocating IP addresses. The guest PC/laptop is configured to obtain an IP address automatically by default, so as soon as it connects to your LAN it will look for a DCHP server and, if you are running one, it will obtain IP address, gateway address for Internet access and so forth, automatically – even when *you* are on holiday.

Most of the combined ADSL modem/router products provide a DHCP server option and a web-based interface to configure it, so even on a peer network you can have the advantages of DHCP. On a client/server system, of course, you can run your DHCP server from your file server box if you wish.

Summary

In this chapter we have considered IP addressing schemes and how best to implement them to meet the operational requirements of your network. We have looked at hubs, switches and routers and the part that they play in expanding your network beyond the two-PC model that we explored in Chapter 1.

We have touched on some aspects of Internet connectivity: the role of the default gateway and DNS. Internet topics are developed further in Chapter 9, *Internet and e-mail*.

07

**fault tolerance
and disaster
recovery**

In this chapter you will learn:

• about backup options

• how to implement a RAID array

• about mains power
  conditioning

7.1 Prepare for the inevitable

Sooner or later, things break. Don't think in terms of *if* a component fails, think about *when*. The day will come (and it could be today) when the main hard disk in your file-sharing PC dies and all the files on it are irretrievably lost. Whether this is a full blown catastrophe or the cause of an extended lunch break for the staff affected is largely a matter of how well you prepared for it.

Fault tolerance

Fault tolerance is concerned with keeping the system going in spite of equipment failures. In large corporations with critical data and the need for 100% uptime this is achieved by building high levels of redundancy into the system. If you are running a bank or an airline, you need high availability for both operational reasons and to preserve customer confidence. This generally involves using 'hot' spares, i.e. if something fails the system will continue to function and the failed spare can be replaced without interruption of service. Obviously this type of availability comes at a price: a load balancing cluster of servers which back up to a remote data centre across a high speed leased communications link, for example, doesn't come cheap.

Disaster recovery

Disaster recovery is at the other end of the cost and availability scale to fault tolerance. It is concerned with restoring data and functionality after a system failure. It accepts that there will be some down-time in the event of an equipment failure and is designed to restore data and functionality within a reasonable time frame. What constitutes reasonable is a judgement that you have to make according to your business needs and priorities. If you had perfect fault tolerance built into your system you wouldn't need disaster recovery at all. However, perfect fault tolerance is a very expensive option, so most of us have to settle for such fault tolerance as we can afford and a level of disaster recovery measures which will meet our operational needs without breaking the bank.

7.2 Backup options

The one thing you cannot afford to lose is data. Hardware, software and entire systems can be replaced, but data, once lost, is lost for good. The single most important aspect of your disaster recovery strategy is an adequate backup system for your data. One of the strongest arguments for using a single PC as a shared file store, whether on a peer network or as part of a client/server system, is the ease and effectiveness of a centralized backup system. This chapter assumes that you are backing up and maintaining a single shared file store machine, though the techniques described could be applied at the level of individual PCs each with a file store area on its (C:) hard disk.

Physical backup media

The physical backup medium may be some form of disk, tape, or flash memory. The key characteristics are that the media should be removable for off-site storage and that data should be restorable from the removable storage medium.

The storage medium that you choose will depend largely on the amount of data that you need to back up.

Pen drives

These are also known as 'thumb drives' or 'gizmo sticks'. They fit in one of your USB ports and after a second or two Windows recognizes them as a removable disk and allocates a drive letter. This means that you can drag and drop files to your removable drive, just as you would any other drive on the system. The storage capacity of these drives varies between 128MB and 2GB. Because of their small size, they are ideal for moving files between machines or as a short-term backup in the absence of anything more organized. Because USB is a cross-platform technology, these drives can be read/written to by other systems such as Apple Mac machines or Linux-based PCs. However, these drives are based on *flash memory* and are not as robust as most of the alternatives.

External hard drives

These are usually standard ATA hard disks, like the main disks in your PC or server, housed in an outer case. The have their own external power supply and usually attach to the system through either a USB or a Firewire port. External drives are available in the standard sizes: 40GB, 80GB, 120GB or more, and like the Pen drives we considered above, they are recognized by Windows when they are plugged in and allocated a drive letter. This means that you can drag and drop files when they are connected and remove the drive for safe storage when not in use.

CD/DVD

CDs usually hold up to 650–700MB and single-sided DVDs hold up to 4.7GB

If you have mainly text files in your business – letters, memos, small spreadsheet applications – you may find that a CD or DVD has enough capacity to store your files.

Windows provides the means of copying to CD/DVD without using third-party software.

To write files to a CD/DVD drive using Windows XP:

1 Right-click on the folder that you want to back up and select the **Send To** option from the context menu.

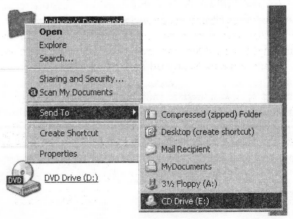

Figure 7.01

2 Providing you have a writable CD/DVD drive attached, choosing **Send To** will put the folder (and its subfolders and files) into a temporary storage area ready to be burnt to the destination drive. When you have done this, Windows displays a balloon at the bottom of the screen. Click in this to open a dialog box to burn the files to the writable drive. An alternative route to this dialog box is to navigate through **My Computer** and click on the writable drive's icon. Either way you will be given the choices shown in Figure 7.02.

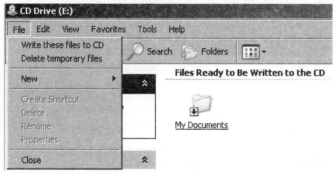

Figure 7.02

3 To write the selected files, select **Write these files to CD** from the **File** menu or, if you change your mind, cancel the operation by selecting **Delete temporary files**.

The process is essentially similar if you are using a Vista PC: use the **Send to** option from the context menu. Alternatively, you can highlight the folders that you want to back up, then select **Burn** from the menu bar at the top of the window (Figure 7.03).

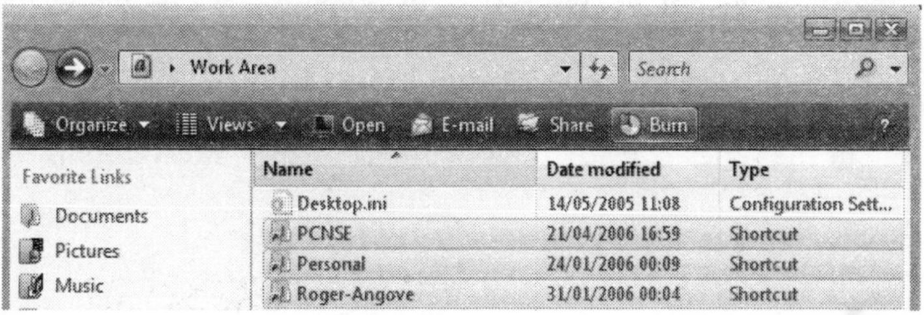

Figure 7.03

Both CD and DVD drives use cross-platform file systems for storing your data, so you can read or recover your data on a different machine type such as a Linux PC or a Mac running MACOS X if you need to.

Tape drives

Various types of tape drives have been used for backing up data for decades. Tape systems of various kinds offer a lot of storage using a well-tried and tested technology. Most drives are available for fitting as internal ATA drives, using the same data cables and power connectors as your existing ATA drives. USB or Firewire connections are also available.

Some frequently used tape/drive types are:

Drive type	Size	Storage capacity
DAT (digital audio tape) cartridge	4mm	1GB–20GB
DLT (digital linear tape)	0.5"	10GB–50GB
Exabyte	8mm	2.5GB–60GB
QIC (quarter inch cartridge)	0.25"	40MB–20GB
Redwood	0.5"	10GB–50GB

DAT and DLT are most often used on desktop PCs with a lot of data and on small server/shared file store machines. The other types are more commonly used on larger systems. What you choose will depend on your present and projected future storage needs and your budget.

As tape drives are almost exclusively used as part of organized backup systems (see the section *Media rotation* below) they can usually be set up to run automatically either using Windows facilities or proprietary software. Common practice is to schedule a backup job to run overnight, to check the following morning that the job has run, then change the tape so that the next one in the series is ready to go without further intervention.

7.3 Backup types

Full backup

As the name suggests, this consists of backing up all data files to removable media suitable for off-site storage. If you are using an automated overnight backup system you can simply do a full backup overnight, every night. This means that in the event of data loss you can restore all data (up to the previous night's backup) from a single tape.

Differential backup

This backs up all files that have been changed since the last full backup. In the event of data loss you can restore all data by restoring the last full backup, followed by restoring the last differential backup, i.e. you need to restore from two tapes (or other storage media) to recover all your backed up data.

Incremental backup

This backs up only those files that have been modified since the last backup of any kind. For example, if you did a full backup on Monday, followed by incremental backups on Tuesday and Wednesday, the Wednesday backup would *not* include files modified on Tuesday. In the event of a failure you would need to restore from three tapes. First you would restore from the full backup that you made on Monday, then from the Tuesday tape to recover files backed up on Tuesday and then from the Wednesday tape and so on until you have restored from the entire series from the last full backup to the last incremental backup.

Media rotation

It is advisable to have more than one backup of your data. If one set of backup media is lost or destroyed, then restoring from an earlier version is considerably better than nothing. The most common rotation system is generally known as *Grandfather, Father, Son*. As the name suggests there are three backups – or if you are using a mixture of full and differential/incremental backups – three backup sets.

For the sake of simplicity, let's assume that you are using a tape drive to back up all your data every day – i.e. a full backup, possibly as an automated overnight job.

1 Make a full backup to tape 1. Label it and store it somewhere safe where it will not be subjected to extremes of temperature, or strong magnetic fields.

2 On day 2 make a further backup to tape 2. Label and store it.

3 On day 3 make a further backup to tape 3. Label and store it.

4 On day 4, overwrite the data of the grandfather tape, tape 1. You have now established a rotating three-tape set: grandfather, father, and son.

Using this system, you will always have a backup that is no more than 24 hours old and two further backups that are 1 and 2 days old respectively. In the event of the last tape being lost, destroyed or corrupted, you can still recover the bulk of your data from one of the earlier tapes. It is good practice to keep at least one generation of the tapes – usually the *Father* tape in secure off-site storage, if only by taking it home. This means that even if your premises are burgled, bombed or struck by lightning, the bulk of your data will survive.

Network backup

As a supplement to backup systems which use various removable media, some people set up a system which copies files from the central file store to another machine on the network. This can be a useful supplement to backing up to removable storage, but it is not a satisfactory substitute for it unless you are able to back up to remote storage. If you really need it, there are companies which will rent you remote storage in secure off-site data centres. A Web search on 'remote data storage' will be sufficient to find a number of companies offering this type of service.

7.4 RAID arrays

The Redundant Array of Inexpensive (or Independent) Disks – RAID – is a fault tolerance technology which can be implemented on any PC, though it is most commonly used on server machines.

The basic idea of RAID is a simple one: write your data to more than one disk, then if one disk in the set fails you can recover your data from the remaining disk(s) in the set.

RAID systems are identified by various levels: RAID 0, RAID 1, RAID 5 and so on. RAID 0 does *not* provide any level of fault tolerance – that is not its purpose – and the higher numbered RAID arrays tend to be complex, expensive and excessive for the needs of small business. RAID 1, however, is a straightforward mirroring system which is relatively simple to implement and to maintain.

A basic implementation of RAID 1 consists of a pair of mirrored disks which appear to the system and to the user as a single disk with a single drive letter. When you save a file to (say) your C: drive it is, in fact, written to a mirrored pair of physical drives so there are always two copies of everything. If one of the mirrored pair of disks fails, replace it with a disk of the same size and restore the data from the still functioning disk.

Hardware RAID

The most efficient way of implementing RAID on your system is through hardware. Some motherboards are equipped with a RAID controller, or you can fit an expansion card in a PCI or PCI-E slot on the motherboard. On-board controllers are usually for Serial ATA (SATA). Expansion cards may support SATA, the older Parallel ATA (PATA) interface or the Small Computer Systems Interface (SCSI) connection.

In terms of technical efficiency these disk/interface types can be ranked:

1 SCSI – fast but expensive.

2 Serial ATA – slower than SCSI but widely available and cheaper.

3 Parallel ATA – the slowest and cheapest option.

Whichever disk type you use, the procedure for setting up your RAID is broadly similar. Install the card in the PCI/PCI-E slot, attach the physical drives, and install the software drivers when prompted.

Most controllers support RAID 0 as well as RAID 1 – make sure that you choose RAID 1, this being the option that implements the mirroring system.

The details of setting up a particular RAID controller and providing drivers for the operating system will vary somewhat between manufacturers and products, so read the manufacturer's installation guide before you start. It is possible to migrate an installed operating system such as Windows from a single drive to a hardware RAID array, but it is a troublesome undertaking. It is much easier to treat this as an opportunity to do a clean install of Windows on your new hardware. See Chapter 8, *Installing Windows*.

Software RAID

Most Linux-based systems – such as those we will look at in Chapter 12, *Client/server networks* – support software RAID. At install time, you choose the RAID type that you want – in our case RAID 1 – and the installer will set the system up as RAID 1. The end result actually boots from the RAID array and so looks and feels like hardware RAID to the user. Windows doesn't support this mode of operation.

7.5 Mains power conditioning

PCs run – directly or indirectly – from the mains power supply. Mains power is alternating current (AC) and is subject to overvoltage and under-voltage fluctuations. PCs need a steady supply of direct current (DC) and this is provided by the PC's power supply unit which does the AC/DC conversion and drops the voltage to 12, 5 and 3 volts as required. However, the PSU is not intended to cope with fluctuations in the AC mains voltage and it can certainly do nothing about a failure of the mains supply.

Surge suppressors

Short periods of over-voltage – *spikes* (measured in nanoseconds) and *surges* (measured in milliseconds) – can cause data loss and corruption and even permanent damage to your hardware. The minimum precaution that you should take on *all* your

PCs – not just servers – is to equip them with a surge suppressor. These may be a simple cube or support several devices. Figure 7.04 shows a 4-way surge protector designed for UK power supplies. Other regions will have their own variants on this.

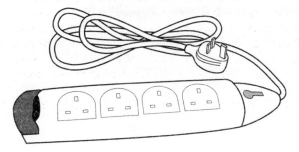

Figure 7.04 A 4-way surge protector.

Surge suppressors of this type are intended to give protection against normal variations in voltage so it its still prudent to shut down and disconnect your equipment in the event of an electrical storm. In the event of a power cut, it may be advisable to disconnect your equipment from the mains supply in case there is a large power surge when power is restored, though this is not vital.

Standby power supplies

In the event of a failure of the mains supply, all of your equipment will cease to work and any open files may be lost or corrupted. A standby power supply – like its grown-up counterpart an uninterruptible power supply – will provide emergency power for long enough to save files and shut down the system in an orderly fashion.

A *standby* or *offline* system has batteries which are continually charged from the mains supply during normal operation in much the same way as a car battery is charged when you are driving. During normal operation the PC draws its power – unconditioned – from the mains supply. When the mains supply fails, the batteries take over. The obvious disadvantages with this are the time that it takes to make the switch from mains to backup batteries – it needs to be fast to prevent problems – and the fact that you need to check the effectiveness of the batteries from time to time. There's not much point in having a standby unit in place and apparently working for months only to find that you have dud batteries just when you need them.

Uninterruptible power supplies

An uninterruptible power supply – also known as an *online* system – has batteries which are charged during normal operation. However, the equipment draws its power from the batteries at all times. This results in a constant supply of clean, conditioned power and if the mains power fails the attached equipment is already running on the batteries so there is no delay in switching supplies. Clearly, this is a more reliable option than a standby system.

Costs and benefits of mains power conditioning

As with nearly everything concerning your system, you need to balance the costs of providing a service and the probable cost of not doing so. It is relatively cheap to provide each PC with a surge protector of some kind and failure to do so could result in data loss or damage to your hardware.

The more expensive options – offline and online – power supplies need to be deployed with care. For example, a laser printer draws a lot of power from the mains, but if the power fails you will only lose the current print job so printers can safely be excluded from your power conditioning arrangements. On the other hand, your main server and your shared file store are vital to your business and will need the best level of protection that you can afford.

Summary

This chapter has looked at the things that will go wrong at some point in your business operation and has suggested some steps that you can take to minimize the impact of equipment failures – to prevent them where possible and to recover from them when they happen. We have considered how to build redundancy into the system with RAID technology and how to condition the mains power to minimize the results of power failure. We have also looked at the rather unglamorous business of backups.

Of all the things that we have considered, however, the most important by far, is to have an effective backup system. If you don't have one, then you are courting disaster. You should have a grandfather/father/son style system which you have tested and at least one data set should be stored off site. Even if every piece of equipment in your office was destroyed overnight it could be replaced, but without data to process you wouldn't have much use for your new data processing equipment – would you?

08 installing windows

In this chapter you will learn:

- how to prepare for a Windows installation

- how to carry out the installation

- how to configure the system

8.1 (Re)installing Windows

There are several reasons why you may want or need to install or reinstall Windows on one or more of your systems:

* Windows has become corrupt, perhaps as a result of a severe virus attack.

* You have to replace the main hard disk in the PC.

* Windows has slowed down after months of continuous use.

The first two reasons are fairly obvious: the PC in question isn't working and the cure is a reinstall of the operating system. The third is, perhaps less easy to spot and, even when spotted, is easy to postpone until next week/after the holidays/when there's more time, etc. However, the fact is, that Windows slows down after a few months of use. The Registry has become filled with junk, the disk is fragmented, there are temporary files here, there and everywhere and whatever you do in terms of maintenance and tuning, the PC never seems to be quite right. In these circumstances the most cost-effective solution may be to format the C: drive and install Windows from first principles.

8.2 Before you start

If you are using a shared file store or a network server there should not be any data stored on the local hard disk. However, users may accidentally save material to their local C: drive so it is worth spending a minute or two checking for locally stored data and backing it up to a removable drive – pen drive, CD, etc. – or copying it to a network drive before disconnecting the workstation PC from the network.

This is also a good time to make sure you have modem/USB/ Ethernet drivers, depending on how you connect to your LAN or to the Internet.

Other things worth noting are the settings for e-mail – server addresses, passwords, etc. – workgroup or domain membership details, and any naming conventions used on the network. All of this information should, of course, be available as part of your network documentation, but a quick check at this point is the work of a few minutes and may save you problems later. Make a note of the workstation's name so that you can restore it in the course of the installation.

In a small company especially, you may like to back up (and later restore) the user's customizations of the system. People often have Desktop wallpaper or screen savers based on personal photos of family members, domestic pets, favourite views, etc. There is no technical reason for doing this, but the amount of goodwill that can be generated by the few minutes of extra work involved can be substantial. If you are the in-house support person in a small company, an ongoing good working relationship with your users can make your day-to-day working life easier and more pleasant. Think of it as one of the more intangible aspects of system maintenance.

Finally, make sure that you have the required Windows installation disks, then disconnect the workstation from the network by unplugging the cable at the back of the PC. What you do next depends on whether your version of Windows is an OEM version or a standard one.

8.3 Installing an OEM version of Windows

The term OEM stands for *Original Equipment Manufacturer*. This term does not indicate the manufacturers of the various components, but the system builder who assembled them into a PC. System builders – particularly the large ones like Dell, or Compaq – often have a licensing agreement with Microsoft to supply a pre-installed version of Windows which is specific to that make and model of PC.

It is not normally considered to be best practice to use this type of operating system release in business because it can be rather inflexible when it comes to the sorts of techniques that we will be considering in Chapter 11, *Building a node*. However, many small businesses do use OEM versions of Windows, mainly because they have been offered a good price when buying a PC which comes with a pre-installed operating system of this type.

This type of OEM version of Windows is usually provided on one (or more) CD disks, labelled something like 'System Restore'. They contain an image of the installed system and are flashed on to the hard drive in order to restore your PC to the state that it was in when it left the factory. When you run a Restore of this type, you will restore the operating system along with any other pre-installed software that may have been bundled with the system. This is a rather inflexible approach, but it has the advantage of being very easy to do.

The first thing to do is to read the instructions. Although there are generic similarities between Restore disks there may be differences of detail between different manufacturers. Generally speaking, however, unless the instructions from the manufacturer state otherwise, put the Restore disk in the CD/DVD drive on your PC, restart it and follow the instructions on screen.

Depending on the speed of your system, the largely automated process of restoring the system may take anything up to an hour. When you are finished, remove the Restore disks and put them somewhere safe – you may need them again one day. Having done this, you will need to restore your backed up data and settings. See the *Post installation procedures* section later in the chapter.

8.4 Installing a standard version of Windows

The OEM versions of Windows are designed to be easy for home users to install in the event of a system failure. Installing a standard version may require a couple of extra preparatory tasks before you start.

Checking CMOS/BIOS settings

Before you start an Operating System install there are a couple of things worth checking in the CMOS setup utility. To do this, reboot the PC and watch the first few screens of information – usually these are white text on a black background because this is happening long before any graphical interface is loaded – and look for a line which says something like '**Press <DEL> to enter SETUP**'. The exact wording will vary from system to system, as will the key required to access the setup menus. The Delete key – DEL – is probably the most frequently used for this purpose, but others such as F2 or F12 are used by some manufacturers.

Once you are in the setup utility, you are interested in two items: the boot order of the PC and the status of CMOS anti-virus checking. Both of these settings can be important for the install process.

If there is an anti-virus function in the CMOS setup and it is set to **Enabled** then change it to **Disabled**. The reason for this is that the Windows Installer will write to system areas of your hard disk as part of the installation process and this could look like virus activity to the anti-virus utility.

The *boot order* is the order in which the system looks at the various drives as it starts up. To boot to, and install from, a CD or DVD disk, the boot order in CMOS needs to be set so that the system looks at the CD or DVD drive first. Figure 8.01 shows how this is done in a setup screen for a *Phoenix* BIOS.

Figure 8.01

To navigate within the setup utility, use the arrow keys to move the cursor (there's no mouse support in most CMOS setup utilities) and other keys as instructed in the Help screens.

In this example, we use the *left* and *right arrow keys* to move along the menu bar and the *up* and *down arrow* keys to move up and down the menus. In Figure 8.01 the CD-ROM drive is second in the list on the **Boot** menu. To make it first, navigate to it then, when it is highlighted, press the [+] key to move it up the list. Any item in the list may be promoted with [+] or demoted with [−]. When you have set the boot order to what you want – in this case CD-ROM, Hard Drive, Removable drive would be ideal – exit from the setup program and save your changes.

Other BIOS manufacturers use their own interfaces to the setup utility, so if you have (say) an AMI or AWARD BIOS they will have the facility to change the boot order but may use entirely different ways of achieving it. Experiment – and don't forget the **Quit without saving** option if you get yourself into a mess.

Starting the installer

Before you start the install, check that you have the product key to install Windows – the disk's packaging should have the key on the back. This is a 25-character code in the form:

XXXXX-XXXXX-XXXXX-XXXXX-XXXXX

You will need it to complete the installation process.

The following example takes you through the process of installing Windows XP Professional – the procedures for installing other Windows versions, such as Vista, are essentially similar.

1   Put the installation disk in the CD or DVD drive and restart your PC. The system will detect the installation disk and prompt you to 'Press any key' to start the installer/boot. Press a key and the display turns from white-on-black to white-on-blue and the system takes a minute or two to load various drivers. When this is done you will see a 'Welcome' screen – white text on a blue background.

2   Press [Enter] to continue with the installation. The system now displays the End User Licence Agreement (EULA).

3   Press [F8] to accept the terms of the EULA and to proceed with the installation.

The next stage of the installation process is to partition and format your hard disk. If this is a clean install on to a new disk the system will show you the amount of free space on the disk and you can install on to this just by accepting default values – i.e. use the whole of the free space and format it with the NTFS file system. If, as in this example, you are doing a reinstall, the system will show you the existing setup.

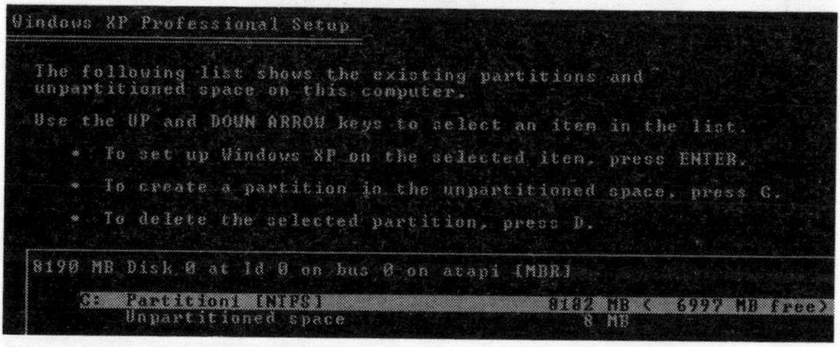

Figure 8.02

In this example, we have a previous installation that we want to remove prior to a new installation.

4 Press [D] to delete this partition. You will receive a warning notice that you are about to remove a system partition – this is what you want to do, so confirm this by pressing [Enter]. You will be asked to confirm (again).

5 Press [L] to continue, followed by [Enter] to install on the newly created free space. You will be asked for format options as shown in Figure 8.03.

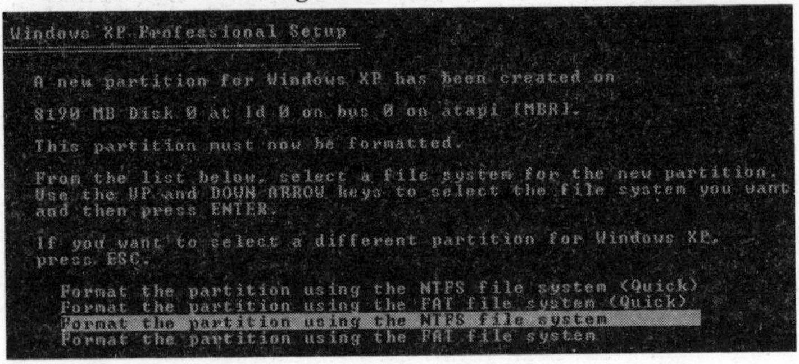

Figure 8.03

6 The default is a full (not a quick) NTFS file system format. Accept this by pressing [Enter]. The system will display a progress bar. Depending on your disk size, and the overall power of your PC this may be several minutes' work – probably enough time to make a cup of tea or coffee.

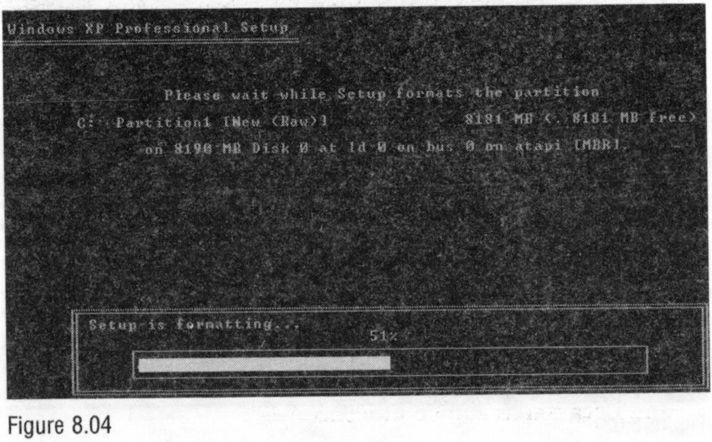

Figure 8.04

When the format is complete, the installer copies files to your hard disk – again this can be a lengthy process – time enough to drink the tea or coffee that you made in the previous step. Progress is monitored and reported by another progress bar. Once the file copy part of the process is finished, the system reboots.

Figure 8.05

After the reboot the system moves to a graphical interface for the remainder of the process which will keep you informed about progress and even give estimates of the time remaining before completion. Treat these estimates with caution.

Figure 8.06

7   The next stage which requires input from you – the user – is the choice of language settings (Figure 8.07). The default is the United States. To change this click on **Customize** and choose the country settings for both **Standard and formats**, and **Location** as shown in Figure 8.08.

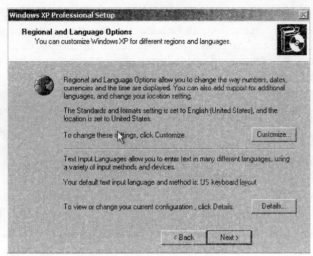

Figure 8.07

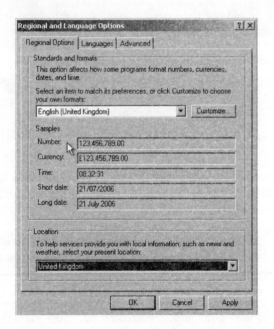

Figure 8.08

8 You should also set the default language and keyboard input options by clicking the **Details** button near the bottom right of the dialog box, shown in Figure 8.07.

9 With these details entered and confirmed, continue by clicking **Next**. You will be prompted to enter a user name – which is mandatory – and an organization name which is optional. Enter the required information and click **Next** to continue.

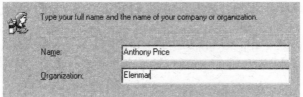

Type your full name and the name of your company or organization.

Na_me: Anthony Price

_Organization: Elenmar

Figure 8.09

The organization name – in this example Elenmar – provides the starting point for the system generated computer name later.

10 You will be asked for the product key. Enter this carefully and click **Next**. If you have made a mistake you will see an error message. If this happens, go back and correct it.

11 The next stage is to give your PC a name – this is optional, but something meaningful or attractive is probably better that the system generated name. Accept or edit this as you wish.

Setup has suggested a name for your computer. If your computer is on a network, your network administrator can tell you what name to use.

_Computer name: ELENMAR-7F3F999

Figure 8.10

12 The next step is to create the Administrator password. This gives access to the local machine – not the network – but it should be protected by a strong password – a mixture of upper and lower case letters, numbers and symbols, such as Fr1day-999. This account should be reserved for admin tasks and not given to users.

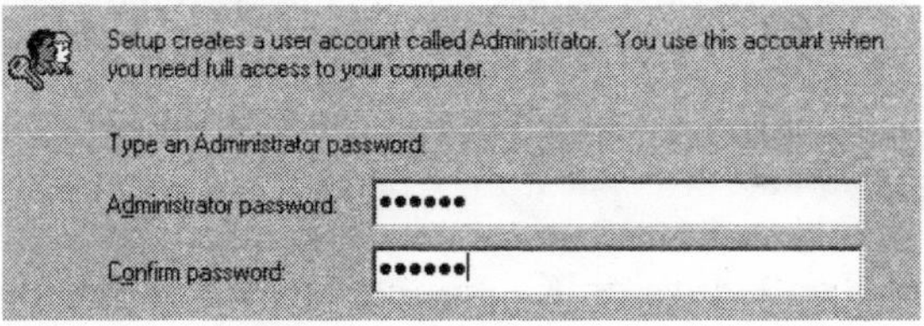

Setup creates a user account called Administrator. You use this account when you need full access to your computer.

Type an Administrator password.

A_dministrator password: ••••••

Co_nfirm password: ••••••

Figure 8.11

13 Click **Next** and you will be prompted to enter your Time Zone. You can also check (and change if necessary) the time and date information for your PC. With this information in place the installer sets up your network settings. Accept the default values in the **Typical Settings** option and click **Next**.

14 You will be asked whether the PC will be part of a domain. Even if you are going to join one later, you can answer 'No' at this point and join your workgroup – here ELENMAR.

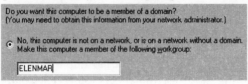

Figure 8.12

15 The installer will now run for some time. It requires no more input from you until after it has rebooted itself. It may then offer to adjust your display settings. Click **OK** to accept this.

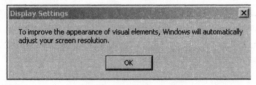

Figure 8.13

16 The next step is to turn on/off Automatic Updates. If you are not connected to the Internet you can set this to *Not right now* and return to it later. Whatever you choose, Windows will display the XP Splash screen while it works in the background before taking you to the Welcome screen and inviting you to 'Spend a few minutes setting up your computer'.

17 You will be presented with the Internet Connection options – skip these and come back to them after you have connected to your LAN. Chapter 9, *Internet and e-mail* looks at this.

18 The next stage is **Activating the product over the Internet**. This is an anti-piracy feature which checks that the installation is from a licensed copy which has not previously been installed on a different PC – you can reinstall it as many times as you like on the same PC. If you are not connected to the

Internet skip this and return to it later. You have 30 days to do this and Windows will remind you from time to time.

19 The next screen prompts you to enter names of people who will be using the PC, to set up user accounts for them. At this point, Windows will insist that you create at least one user account and by default, this will have full administrative privileges. Create an account called 'user' and continue with the installation. We will return to the business of creating and securing user accounts as part of the following section. Once you have added your new account, click **Next** and the system will confirm that you have finished.

8.5 Post-installation procedures

Remove any installation disks from the PC's drives and put them away somewhere safe. Reconnect the network cable and reboot the PC. The first thing that you will notice is that the PC boots to the default user Desktop and the user 'user' is logged on automatically without having to provide a password. This may be acceptable for home use, but in a business, even where you are not using a client/server domain-based network you need better security than this. If yours is a domain-based network, follow the procedures below, otherwise skip forward to the *Connecting to a workgroup* section, page 121.

Connecting to a domain

If you have a domain-based network, now is the time to connect to the domain controller. You will need network administrator privileges to do this.

1 Right-click on the **My Computer** icon and select **Properties**.

2 Choose the **Computer name** tab.

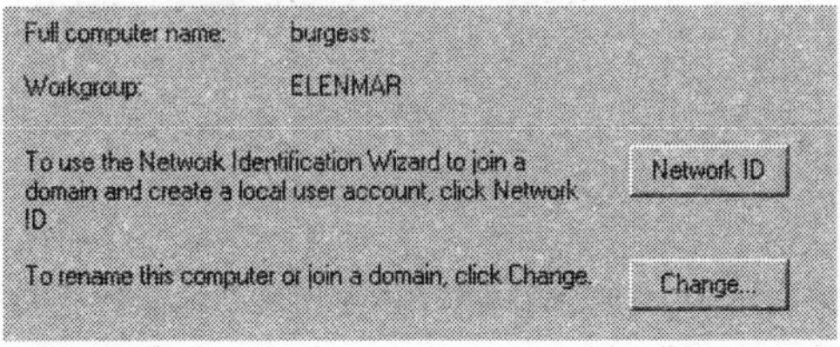

Figure 8.14

3 Click **Change**. This will show the current name of the PC and the name of the workgroup to which it belongs.

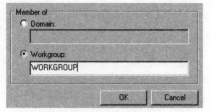

Figure 8.15

4 Select the **Domain** radio button and enter your domain name.

5 Click **OK**. You will be presented with a logon dialog box for the *network* administrator account. In this example, we are joining a domain where this account is called 'admin' – on other network systems it may be called 'root' or 'superuser'.

Figure 8.16

6 Enter the required name and password. Click on **OK**. After a few seconds you will receive a welcome message.

7 Click on **OK** to join the named domain. You will then receive a message telling you to reboot the PC. Click **OK**.

Because of the nature of a domain-based system, user logons, authentication and security will all be taken care of by the domain controller. When the PC restarts, you, or the user, will see the standard Windows logon screen where you can log on to any existing account.

For more on domain-based systems, see Chapter 12, *Client/server networks*.

Connecting to a workgroup shared file store

A workgroup is, by its nature, less secure than a domain-based system, so we need to take a few steps to bring the security up to a reasonable standard. We can accomplish this by tweaking our user accounts and settings. We looked at how to create and modify user accounts in Chapter 2 under the heading of *Setting up user accounts* on page 15. Refer back to this section if necessary, then do the following.

1   Create a strong password for the user account that you set up during the installation. Ideally this should be something that is easy for you to remember, but difficult for anyone else to guess. It should also contain a mixture of upper and lower case letters, numbers and symbols.

2   Create an account for each real user and assign a password.

3   Set each real user account to the Limited type.

Creating and modifying an account

In this example we will create a new user account for the user Anthony, password protect it and give it restricted privileges.

1   Navigate to **Control Panel > User Accounts.**

2   Click on **Create a new account.**

Pick a task...

* Change an account

* Create a new account

* Change the way users log on or off

Figure 8.17

3   Give the new account a name.

Name the new account

Type a name for the new account:

Anthony

Figure 8.18

4   Change the account type to **Limited.**

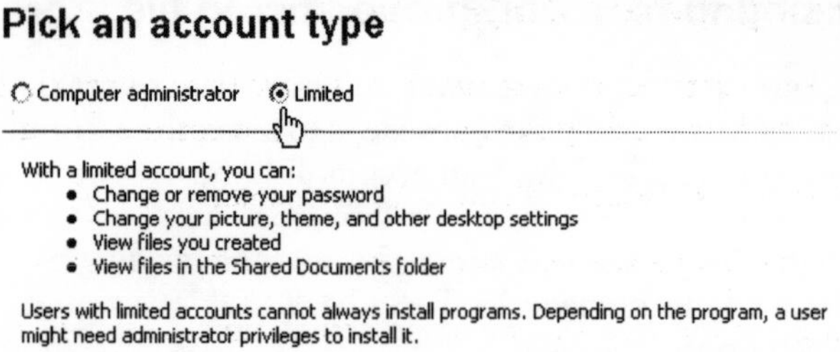

Pick an account type

○ Computer administrator   ● Limited

With a limited account, you can:
- Change or remove your password
- Change your picture, theme, and other desktop settings
- View files you created
- View files in the Shared Documents folder

Users with limited accounts cannot always install programs. Depending on the program, a user might need administrator privileges to install it.

Figure 8.19

5   Return to the **User accounts** section and click on the account you wish to change – in this case Anthony – and select the **Create a password** option.

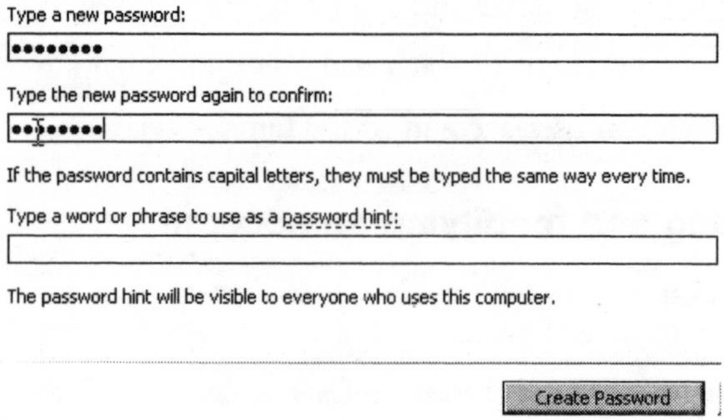

Type a new password:

`••••••••`

Type the new password again to confirm:

`••••••••`

If the password contains capital letters, they must be typed the same way every time.

Type a word or phrase to use as a password hint:

The password hint will be visible to everyone who uses this computer.

Create Password

Figure 8.20

6   Type in the new password for this user, confirm the new password and click on the **Create password** button.

7   When you have finished, close the User accounts window to return to the Control Panel.

Note that the owner of the new Limited account will still have control over personal settings such as their password, Desktop settings and so on but will be unable to make system-wide changes or install new software. This is useful from a security point of view – system changes and software installation should only be done from an administrator account and even the administrator should also have a limited account for day-to-day work.

If you have more than one user who requires an account on this PC, go through steps 1–6 above for each user.

Securing the log on process

With your user accounts in place, it is now time to get rid of the security hole caused by the automatic logon for the default user.

1   Navigate to **Control Panel > User accounts**.

2   Select **Change the way users log on or off**.

3   Uncheck the **Use the welcome screen** box. This will disable the Welcome screen and Fast User Switching. Click **Apply options**.

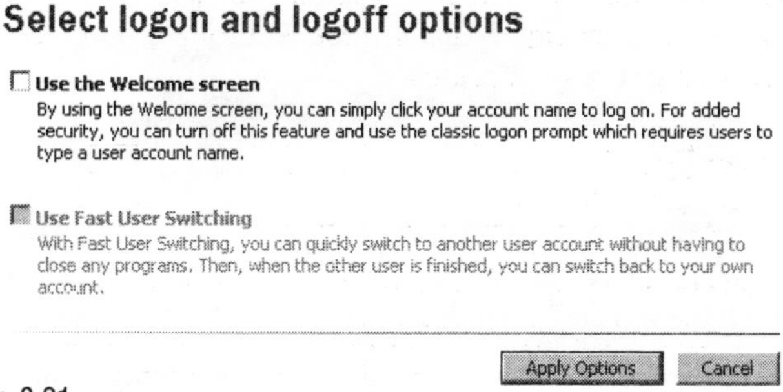

Select logon and logoff options

☐ **Use the Welcome screen**
By using the Welcome screen, you can simply click your account name to log on. For added security, you can turn off this feature and use the classic logon prompt which requires users to type a user account name.

☐ **Use Fast User Switching**
With Fast User Switching, you can quickly switch to another user account without having to close any programs. Then, when the other user is finished, you can switch back to your own account.

[Apply Options]   [Cancel]

Figure 8.21

This means that users will be presented with the standard Windows logon screen at start-up time.

Redirecting My Documents

The final step in preparing the new system for your users is to redirect the Desktop **My Documents** icon to the shared file store.

For each user account on the system:

1   Log on as that user.

2   Right-click on the My Documents icon and select **Properties**. This shows the current location of the *My Documents* folder.

Target folder location
Target: C:\Documents and Settings\Anthony\My Docume

[Restore Default]   [Move...]   [Find Target...]

Figure 8.22

3   Click **Move**, then navigate to the folder you want to use.

Figure 8.23

4   Click **OK** to confirm this new location. You will be given the option to move files to the new location if you want to. When you have finished, Windows will show the new location.

With the new user accounts in place and *My Documents* redirected, your users may now access the LAN. They should be encouraged to change the password which you allocated for something known only to them. This is a minimal security policy. More effective policies are considered in Chapter 14, *Security*.

8.6 Mapping a network drive

Although you can set and use a path to My Documents – or any other folder – across your network, it can be convenient to allocate a drive letter to it. To do this:

1   Open any folder on your PC.

2   Select **Tools > Map Network Drive** from the menu.

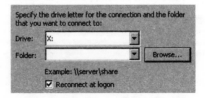

Figure 8.24

3 Click **Browse,** navigate to a shared folder and click **OK.** The system will display the path to the target and the drive letter allocated to it. By default, the system will reconnect at start-up. With your drive mapped, you can refer to it by its drive letter rather than using the path to it.

Summary

In this chapter we have seen how to install (or reinstall) Windows from either OEM Restore disks or from a standard installation disk. We have looked in some detail at the procedures as they apply to XP Professional edition, and noted that other Windows versions are broadly similar though they may differ in detail.

We have seen how to set up and password-protect user accounts and how to redirect the user accounts to a shared file store – a revision and extension of these topics which were introduced in Chapter 2. We also considered some security basics concerning passwords and noted that the topic of security will be considered further in Chapter 14.

09

internet and e-mail

In this chapter you will learn:

- how to connect to the Internet
- how to activate and update Windows
- about Internet and e-mail security
- how to check the speed of your Internet connection

9.1 Setting up an Internet connection

To connect to the Internet you need an access account with an Internet Service Provider (ISP) and a physical connection through a modem or a router. Your ISP will provide you with a user name and a password – make sure you have these to hand when you start to set up your connection. Many ISPs provide a broadband modem as part of their broadband package. Setting up and sharing a modem has been outlined in Chapter 2, *Sharing resources* and while this may be acceptable where you want to share a connection between a couple of PCs, most small businesses can benefit from using a broadband modem/router. This has the advantage of being always available without relying on one of your PCs to provide the connection-sharing and not imposing any overhead on the PC workstation that is used for the Internet connection.

9.2 Installing a broadband modem/router

Settings and equipment check

As with all equipment installation you should check that you have all necessary cables and connectors and that you have read any installation instructions from the manufacturer. In particular you will need to know some settings which will be provided by your ISP. These are:

+ User name: *yourusername@yourisp*
+ Password: *nnnnnnn*

Other settings you may need for your router.

+ Encapsulation: PPPoA
+ Multiplexing: VC Based
+ VPI: 0
+ VCI: 38

You don't need to know what these settings mean – just have them to hand and enter them when – or if – necessary. (Note: the values in the example reflect UK experience and will vary according to the country where you are doing the setting up.) The other thing that you will need is the router's default IP address – this will be in the router's manual or set up instructions. The default IP address in the example that follows is 192.168.2.1 – this may be different if you are using a different make or model of router/modem.

Connecting your router

1 Connect all cables. There will be one from the Ethernet port on your PC to one of the ports on the router; there will be another from the router to the splitter which connects both router and telephone to the phone line. With these two in place, connect the router to its power supply. Various lights on the router will flicker as it runs though its power-on self-test/boot sequence.

2 When the router has settled down you will have a power indicator to show that it is powered up, along with some others for the ADSL side of the connection. The port to which you have connected the Ethernet cable should be showing a steady light to indicate that the connection is in place. Ports which have no cable attached will not show lights. If there are any problems at this stage – unlikely – then check cable connections and power and have a look at the router manual or setup instructions.

3 With all the hardware in place and powered up, the next thing to do is to configure the modem/router through its web interface. To do this, start your web browser – Firefox, Internet Explorer or whatever – and type in the default IP address of your router. You don't need any 'http' or 'www' just the numeric IP address in the browser bar as shown in Figure 9.01 and press [Enter].

Figure 9.01

4 The browser will add the http:// prefix for you and you will be taken to the login screen for the router. As this is the first time you have accessed the router there won't be a password

in place – or if there is, it will be a default password which will be shown in the product documentation. The login screen for the router will look something like Figure 9.02.

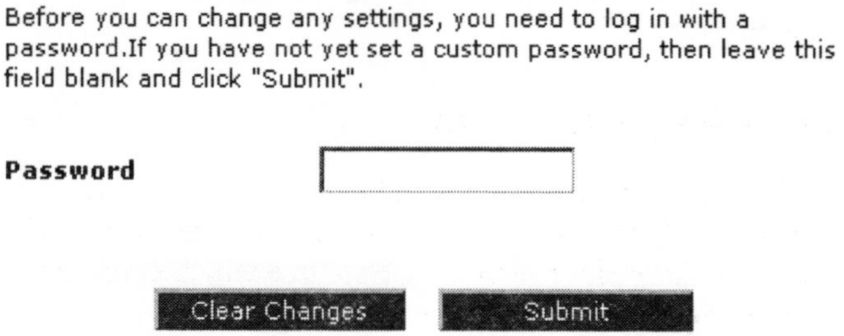

Before you can change any settings, you need to log in with a password. If you have not yet set a custom password, then leave this field blank and click "Submit".

Password

Clear Changes   Submit

Figure 9.02

5   Enter a password, if necessary, and press [**Enter**]. The Welcome screen will list the options, including Setup Wizard.

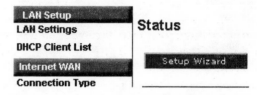

LAN Setup
LAN Settings
DHCP Client List
Internet WAN
Connection Type

Status

Setup Wizard

Figure 9.03

6   Click on this and step through the setup options one by one, entering the information from your ISP as necessary.

7   In this example, the default **Connection Type** is PPPoE – change it to PPPoA as shown in Figure 9.04 and click **Next**.

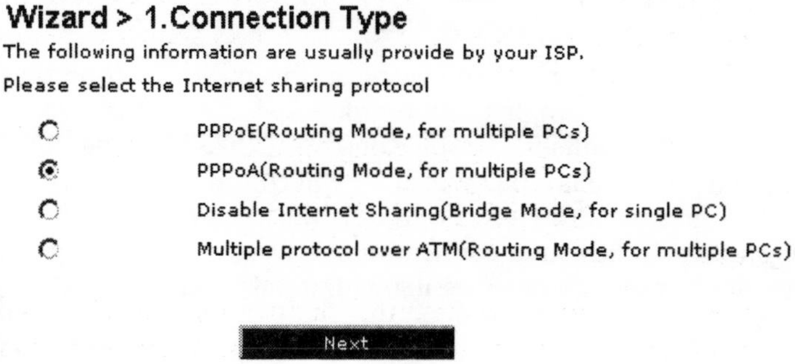

Wizard > 1. Connection Type

The following information are usually provide by your ISP.

Please select the Internet sharing protocol

○   PPPoE(Routing Mode, for multiple PCs)

◉   PPPoA(Routing Mode, for multiple PCs)

○   Disable Internet Sharing(Bridge Mode, for single PC)

○   Multiple protocol over ATM(Routing Mode, for multiple PCs)

Next

Figure 9.04

8 At the next screen, enter your user name and password and the values for VPI/VCI as supplied by your ISP.

The following information are usually provided by your ISP.

> **Username:**   efh9999@efhbb.cc

> **Password:**   ●●●●●●●

> **Retype Password:**   ●●●●●●●

> **VPI/VCI:**   0   /   38

Back   Next

Figure 9.05

9 Click **Next**. The Wizard will show you a summary screen.

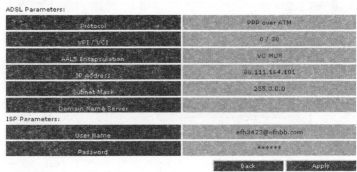

ADSL Parameters:

Protocol	PPP over ATM
VPI / VCI	0 / 38
AAL5 Entapsulation	VC MUX
IP Address	86.111.164.101
Subnet Mask	255.0.0.0
Domain Name Server	

ISP Parameters:

User Name	efh3423@efhbb.com
Password	******

Back   Apply

Figure 9.06

10 Check that the information is correct, then click **Apply**. The router will save your settings and reboot – this may take half a minute or so. Your router should now be working. Check by pointing your browser at a website.

With the router in place and working, this may be a good time to go back to the configuration utility and check other system settings – these will include some options such as blocking PING requests from the Internet which we will consider later when we look at firewalls. You now need to set the password for controlling access to the router configuration screens – having set it up, you don't want any one messing with it – do you?

If your browser won't connect

If your browser can't see the router then it is probably a problem with the network settings on your PC. Navigate to the **Network Connections** applet in the **Control Panel**, right-click on **Properties**. Select the **Internet Protocol** item in the list and click on the **Properties** button. Make sure that your PC is set up to obtain an IP address automatically.

9.3 Activating and updating Windows

If this is the first time that you have connected a new installation of Windows to the Internet you may need to activate the newly-installed operating system and you will almost certainly need to update it.

Activating Windows

Not everyone will need to do this. Most OEM versions of Windows are customized so that they can only be installed on the original hardware and don't require activation. There are also volume licensing versions of Windows – mainly used by larger companies – which are exempt from the requirement to activate them. However, a fresh install of a standard version of Windows needs to be activated within 30 days of installation. This can be done over the phone by reading a 50-digit identification key to a customer service representative then entering a 42-digit confirmation ID which they will dictate to you. For obvious reasons, most people prefer to use the automated process on the Internet.

A fresh install of Windows that has not been activated will remind you from time to time by displaying a balloon and a message in the system tray. Alternatively, click on the **Start** button and choose the **Activate Windows** shortcut at the top of the **All Programs** menu. The activation process is almost always automatic. You don't need to provide any licensing or other information – just point, click and wait a few seconds and you will receive a confirmation message. If the activation process doesn't work, you will need to telephone Microsoft and activate manually.

How Windows product activation works

Versions of Windows prior to XP were relatively easy to duplicate illegally so Microsoft introduced product activation to make sure that you only installed your version of Windows on one PC. During the activation process, Windows generates and transmits a 'fingerprint' based on your hardware components. When you reinstall on the *same hardware* the 'fingerprint' will match the previous one stored in the activation database. However, if you have made significant changes to your hardware since the initial activation, or you attempt to install on to a different PC, the fingerprint files won't match and the attempt at activation will be rejected. This can happen for quite innocent reasons and you can telephone Microsoft and they will help you to sort out the problem. Also if you reinstall and activate within 120 days of the last activation you may have to ring MS; likewise if major hardware is changed often within the first 120 days, XP issues a re-activate notice and gives you three days to do this.

Updating Windows

Like all operating systems, Windows is in a constant state of development and various upgrades, fixes and security patches are available over the Internet. To make sure that your installed version is fully up to date, use the Windows Update service. Any of the following should work:

+ Type *wupdmgr* at a system prompt or in a Run box (XP only).

+ If you use the Internet Explorer browser choose the **Update** option from the **Tools** menu.

+ Point your browser to **http://windowsupdate.microsoft.com**.

+ **Start > All programs > Windows update** (top of column).

Once you are at the Windows Update site, just follow the instructions on screen to update your system.

You can set Automatic Update options through the Windows Control Panel.

9.4 Internet and e-mail security basics

Anti-virus measures

If you connect any PC to the Internet without a fully functioning and up-to-date anti-virus package in place, then you will probably pick up some sort of malicious program – virus, trojan, worm, whatever – in a matter of hours (if not minutes). Even before product activation or running the Windows Update service, you should make sure that you have installed *and updated* an anti-virus package.

If you are using a client/server network, the first line of defence is anti-virus software running on the server. Many, if not most, of the anti-virus software vendors provide software that will run on Windows or Linux servers, both file servers and mail servers. Automated updates are available for most systems, so provided these are in place and working, your first line of defence is in place and requires no input from your users.

Individual workstation PCs on your network should also run their own anti-virus packages and these can usually be automatically updated from the local server on a client/server network. Where you are using a peer network, you may need to configure each workstation's anti-virus software to automatically update from the Internet. If you choose this option, make sure that you set up automatic updates to run overnight and/or at boot time. Do *not* rely on your users to do this – it only needs one person to forget or to get it wrong and the whole of your network may become infected.

Firewalls

When you connect to the Internet you are starting a two-way communication process. When you click on a link or type a web address in a browser bar you are requesting information to be sent to you. Unfortunately, there is nothing to stop anyone from sending you material that you have not requested unless you have some means of preventing this. The answer to this problem is a firewall – an electronic door keeper which monitors traffic between your LAN and the wider world of the Internet.

Hardware firewalls

These are devices which stand between your network and the outside world. They vary between enterprise-level devices from the big names such as Cisco Systems and at the other end of the scale a simple barrier built into a combined ADSL modem/router. Whichever system you use, the fundamental principle is the same – all Internet requests originating from your LAN are sent via the firewall box. The firewall box has two IP addresses – a public address which is visible on the Net and a private one that is part of your private network. Each request from one of your workstation PCs is sent to the firewall box instead of directly to the Internet. The firewall device requests the page using its public address and notes the private address of the PC making the request. When a reply is received from the Internet, the firewall checks its record of requests from local addresses and if, and only if, the incoming data packets were requested from one of your local network PCs is the data allowed in. Unsolicited data packets may be rejected, but more commonly they are silently ignored or dropped. If you are using an ADSL modem/router, you can generally turn on the firewall through the web-based interface which you use to set up and control the device.

Figure 9.07 shows the Enable/Disable choice for a hardware firewall of this type. Obviously, large (and expensive) enterprise level devices will give a greater degree of granularity of control, though even a simple device such as this will allow you to open specific ports if you need to do so. For example, you may want to allow a particular piece of software to access the Internet on a particular PC. To do this, you need to open a port on your firewall and map it to the IP address of the PC that needs access.

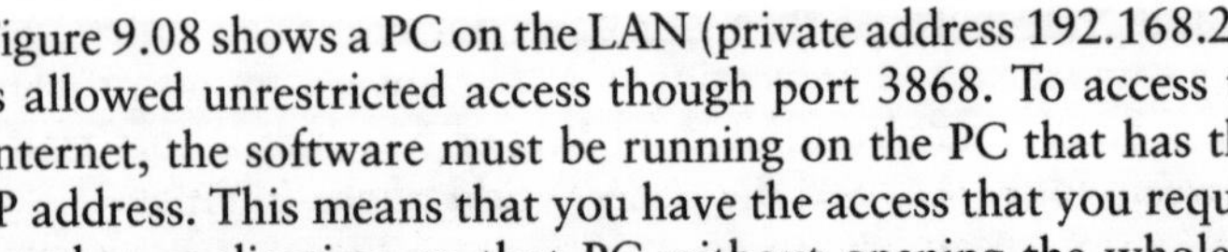

Firewall Enable / Disable > ⦿ Enable ○ Disable

[Clear Changes]   [Apply Changes]

Figure 9.07

Figure 9.08 shows a PC on the LAN (private address 192.168.2.6) is allowed unrestricted access though port 3868. To access the Internet, the software must be running on the PC that has that IP address. This means that you have the access that you require for that application on that PC without opening the whole of your LAN to the possibility of intrusion. However, any open port is like an unlocked door in your house: a small, but nevertheless real security hole. In general you should only open ports for a good reason and check your security status from time to time. (See *Testing your firewall*, page 136.)

No.	LAN IP Address	Protocol Type	LAN Port	Public Port	Enable
1	192.168.2.6	TCP&UDP	3868	3868	☑

Figure 9.08

Software firewalls

These vary from the Windows firewall that is included with XP (Service Pack 2 or later) and Vista, to specialized products which run on their own dedicated PC. Software firewalls allow you to control Internet access by programs running on your network. Obviously, your web browsers and e-mail clients will need to access the Net so they will need permission from the firewall to do this. The general principle is to deny access to all applications by default, then to grant permissions – temporarily or permanently – when the application requests access. Figure 9.09 shows the Windows firewall processing a request.

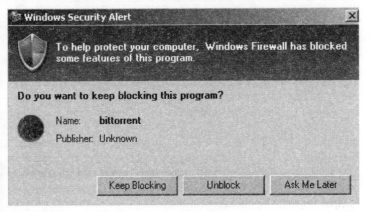

Figure 9.09

There are other software firewalls available and, like their hardware counterparts, they vary in price and the level of control that they give you over Internet access. From the point of view of administration, the ideal is to have a single gateway computer which is firewall protected. If everyone on the LAN connects to the Internet solely through this machine then your entire network is firewalled, i.e. you do *not* need additional firewalling on individual PCs and you can safely disable the Windows firewall which is on by default after an operating system install.

Testing your firewall

Just as you probably test your fire and burglar alarms from time to time so it is good practice to test the effectiveness of your firewall. It's better for you to find a security vulnerability and fix it than for an intruder to find and exploit it. The Gibson Research Corporation provides a free service called *Shields Up* through their site at www.grc.com. If you visit this site and navigate to the Shields Up utility, it will scan your system and report the status of your ports.

Figure 9.10

Figure 9.10 shows part of a port scan. The numbers to the left and right of the figure are port numbers and the darker coloured block indicates that one of the ports – in this case port 80 – responded to the probe. Port 80 is the standard port for a web server, so if the site concerned was running a web server we would expect to see this. However, if the site was not running a web server, we would need further investigation after the port had been closed. You should only open a port for a particular purpose and that purpose should be known and documented as part of your LAN documentation.

The GRC website is well known and widely respected in the industry and has huge amounts of information about security issues. Not all 'security sites' and services are as reliable as this, so (as with most things on the Net) proceed with caution.

Spyware and adware

These take many forms. They may hijack your web browser, display unwanted pop-up advertisements, track which web sites you have visited and so on. Some of the nastier examples of this malware may record keystrokes as you enter private details such as user identities and passwords in an attempt at identity theft.

Whereas viruses, trojans, etc. are merely malicious and destructive, the nastier end of the spectrum of spyware and adware is concerned with financial gain. This means that the resources employed tend to be more professional and faster developing than those involved in virus writing. This type of nuisance is frequently acquired by clicking on a link on a website or responding to free offers – anything from a free competition to win a plasma TV to a free scan to detect spyware. The general rule, then, is to treat everyone with initial suspicion and to encourage your users to do the same.

The answer to spyware and adware is to install, and regularly update and use an appropriate software package. A web search on the term 'spyware' will provide a lot of information about this rapidly changing area of Internet activity. Depending on the way you have set up your network you may want to install an anti-spyware package on your server as well as independent installations on your workstations. Unlike virus checkers, where mixing different products on the same system can cause problems, it is common practice to run more than one anti-spyware package, on the principle that what one package doesn't detect, another will. Many of these products are free or have trial versions available.

9.5 Mail servers

If you have a domain name www.mycompany.com you will probably have – or be able to acquire – an e-mail service with a set of addresses in the form *myname@mycompany.com*. The easiest way for the small business is to subscribe to a package of this kind which is hosted by the supplier. This means that you don't have to run any kind of mail server from your own network or have any ports open in your firewall. The security advantages of this are obvious.

Another advantage of having a fully hosted e-mail solution is the level of security implemented by the service providers. These are usually large companies with secure data centres and it is in their interests to have spam and virus detection mechanisms in place. Many e-mail packages have an option to subscribe to additional anti-spam and anti-virus measures for each of your hosted mailboxes for an annual fee. Even if you don't subscribe to these additional services you will probably benefit from the high levels of security and filtering that are normally associated with large companies' mail operations.

The common mail protocols – SMTP and POP3

For most of us, there are two major e-mail protocols and server types: the Simple Mail Transfer Protocol (SMTP) and the Post Office Protocol (POP3). SMTP is used for sending mail and transporting it across the many servers of the Internet, whereas POP3 is the commonest way of retrieving mail from a mail server. To use these protocols, you will need to configure the mail client program on each of the workstations with details of the SMTP and POP3 servers. You will also need user names and password for each mail account.

E-mail clients

Most businesses use the Microsoft *Outlook* mail program which is part of the Microsoft Office suite. Others may use *Outlook Express* which is supplied with the XP operating system or its upgraded counterpart in Vista, *Windows Mail*. There are, of course, other e-mail packages, many of them free, such as *Thunderbird*, *Kaufmann Mail Warrior* or *Iscribe*. A web search on any of these names will provide details.

Setting up Outlook mail

This example walks through the process of configuring an installed version of Outlook. (Installing a free alternative – *Thunderbird* – is covered in Chapter 10, *Installing applications*.)

1 Click the Outlook icon to launch the application. If there are no e-mail accounts configured on the system you will see a Welcome screen.

Welcome to the Outlook 2003 Startup wizard, which will
guide you through the process of configuring Outlook
2003.

Figure 9.11

2 Click **Next** to run the setup wizard.

3 When prompted to set up an e-mail account, select the radio
button for Yes – the default value – and click **Next**.

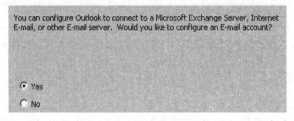

You can configure Outlook to connect to a Microsoft Exchange Server, Internet
E-mail, or other E-mail server. Would you like to configure an E-mail account?

   ⦿ Yes

   ○ No

Figure 9.12

4 At the next screen choose **POP3**, then click **Next**.

5 At the next screen – the main setup screen – enter all of the
details of the e-mail account that you wish to set up.

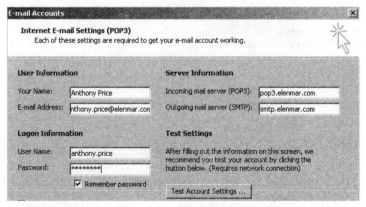

E-mail Accounts   ✕

  Internet E-mail Settings (POP3)
  Each of these settings are required to get your e-mail account working.

User Information

| Your Name: | Anthony Price |
| E-mail Address: | nthony.price@elenmar.con |

Logon Information

User Name:	anthony.price
Password:	**********
	☑ Remember password

Server Information

| Incoming mail server (POP3): | pop3.elenmar.com |
| Outgoing mail server (SMTP): | smtp.elenmar.com |

Test Settings

After filling out the information on this screen, we
recommend you test your account by clicking the
button below. (Requires network connection)

Test Account Settings ...

Figure 9.13

6 When you have entered the necessary information click **Test
Settings**. If you have entered correct values in each of the

fields (and you are connected to the Internet) you will receive confirmation that all is well.

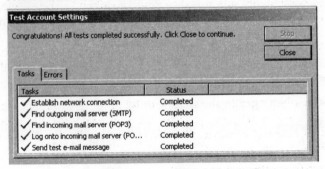

Figure 9.14

7 If you have set up the Outlook mail client correctly, fine, close the test report window, click **Next**, then click **Finish.** If there are errors, now is the time to go back, correct them and try again.

If there is an existing e-mail account that you wish to modify or you wish to add a new e-mail account, start Outlook and use **Tools > E-mail Accounts...** This will start the setup wizard.

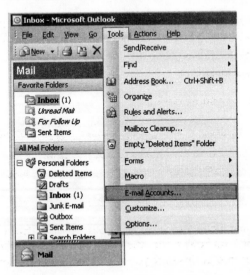

Figure 9.15

Checking the speed of your ADSL connection

When you initially subscribed to your broadband (ADSL) Internet connection, one of the choices that you made was for the connection speed. A basic (10 speed) connection is rated at 512Kbps, with 2Mbps (2,000Kbps) and 8Mbps becoming increasingly common. Doubtless even higher speeds will rapidly become available.

As with anything in business, it is useful to be able to make sure that you are in fact getting what you are paying for and there are a number of free services which help you to do just that. One of these services is at:

http://www.dslreports.com/stest

To use the service, you need a suitable version of Java installed on your system. There is a link on the site which enables you to do this. Click on it and you will receive an almost instant report.

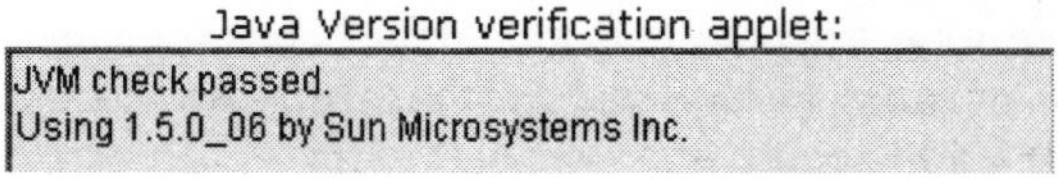

Java Version verification applet:

JVM check passed.
Using 1.5.0_06 by Sun Microsystems Inc.

Figure 9.16

If the report confirms that you have a suitable installation of Java, you can proceed to the speed test. If not, you can click on a link to the Java download site at:

http://java.com/en/

and download and install it.

Figure 9.17

With Java installed, you can now choose a server from the web page and click on **Start** to run the test. This will take a minute or so and at the end of this time you will see a report that looks like Figure 9.18.

dslreports.com speed test result on 2006-07-31
05:25:57 EST:
453 / 236
Your download speed : 453 kbps or 56.6 KB/sec.

Your upload speed : 236 kbps or 29.5 KB/sec.

Figure 9.18

In this instance, the test shows 453Kbps/236Kbps – this being the download and upload speeds actually achieved on this test. However, as with any performance or benchmark test, it pays to run it three or more times just to be sure that the results are typical.

Summary

In this chapter we have extended the simple modem sharing outlined in Chapter 2, *Sharing resources*, to setting up a modem/router. We have considered the needs for activating a new installation of Windows and the procedures necessary to update and secure it.

We have looked at hardware and software firewalls, anti-virus software, and precautions against other forms of malware. We have considered the fundamentals of e-mail provision.

We have seen how to monitor firewall ports and how to test the speed of an Internet connection by using free remote probing services from the Internet.

In this chapter you will learn:

- how to install and configure an office suite

- how to install and configure a web browser

- how to install and configure an e-mail client program

10.1 Installing software

With your operating system installed and security measures in place, you need to set up the basic productivity tools for your users: office software, a browser, and an e-mail client. In this chapter we will look at examples of some of these types of package. The general principles involved are much the same, irrespective of the software vendor. However, as a small (and cost-conscious) business you may like to evaluate some of the free alternatives to the more widely known Microsoft products.

10.2 Open Office

This is a free Open Source office suite designed as a rival to its better known Microsoft counterpart.

The components of the Open Office suite are:

*   **Writer** – a full featured word processor, compatible with Microsoft Word and with a broadly similar user interface.

*   **Impress** – a presentation package which is similar in its functionality to Microsoft's PowerPoint. It is file-compatible with PowerPoint.

*   **Math** – mainly used as an equation editor in text documents.

*   **Draw** – a drawing program. Ideal for flow charts and network diagrams.

*   **Calc** – a spreadsheet package which will be familiar in its workings if you are used to Microsoft's Excel. Files can be saved in Excel format for sharing with Microsoft users.

*   **Base** – a database management tool which allows you to create and query database tables, etc. File-compatible with many (including Microsoft) file formats.

Open Office may not have all of the advanced features of the Microsoft product, but it comes with a zero price tag and has sufficient features for many small businesses. This book was written using the Open Office word processor, and the spreadsheet package was the key to keeping track of chapter lengths and revisions.

Downloading Open Office

You may occasionally find Open Office on magazine cover disks, but the easiest way to make sure that you have the very latest version is to download it from the Open Office site at www.openoffice.org. The English language version of the installer for Windows (there are versions for just about every operating system) is just over 92MB and in a recent test it downloaded in around 25 minutes using an ageing PIII PC on a 512Kbps broadband connection. Obviously if you have a faster connection you can expect to do better than this.

Installing Open Office

With the download complete, install the suite like this:

1　Click on the icon for the installer to start it running. You will be greeted with a 'Thank you' screen.

2　Click **Next** to continue.

3　Accept the default location for the temporary installer files, then click **Unpack**. The installer will spend a few seconds – no more than half a minute – uncompressing the installation files. When this is complete you will see the Welcome screen for the setup program. (Note, by the way, the *Sun Microsystems* logo. Open Office is an Open Source community project but it also has some big name sponsorship.)

4　Click **Next**, accept the licence agreement and click **Next** again.

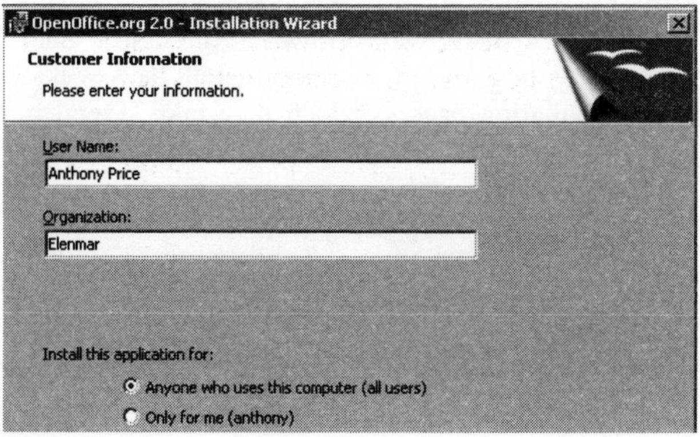

Figure 10.01

5 Fill in user details, allow all users to use the application, then click **Next**. The next screen will give you a choice of a complete or a custom setup. What you choose here depends on what you want from the Open Office suite, but for purposes of this example we will look at what is available through the **Custom Setup**. Whatever your choice, click **Next**.

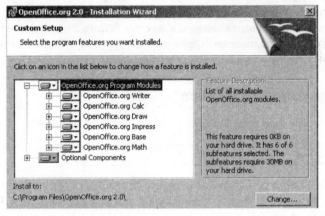

Figure 10.02 Custom Setup options.

6 With the Custom Setup you will see a list of the Open Office components and have the opportunity to change the installation folder. Unless you have good reason to do so, accept the default folder, select the components to install, then click **Next**.

7 The next choice will depend on how you want to use Open Office. If you intend to use it as a replacement for Microsoft products, tick the boxes as shown in the figure. Click **Next**, then, at the next screen, click on **Install**. This will start the main installation process which may take several minutes. The installer outputs progress reports as it goes.

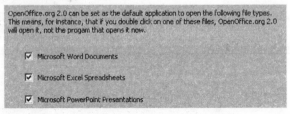

Figure 10.03 Setting file associations.

8 At the end, click **Finish** to exit from the installer.

With the installation process complete it is now safe to delete the temporary files which the installer unpacked at Step 3 above.

Registering Open Office

After the installer has finished you will be returned to your Desktop. The installer will have updated the **Start > Programs** menu. If you have installed all the Open Office components this will look like this:

Figure 10.04

(This may be a good time to create Desktop shortcuts or to use the **Pin to the Start menu** option to enable quick access to the components that you or your users will use frequently.)

As you would expect, clicking on a component will launch it. No matter which component you choose, the first time you use an Open Office program, the registration process will be launched.

1 Click **Next** – this will start the registration for the whole suite – you don't have to do it separately for each component.

2 Read the licence agreement and accept it by clicking **Accept**.

3 Add your user name and initials and click **Next**.

Welcome to OpenOffice.org 2.0	
Steps	**Provide your full name and initials below**
1. Welcome	The user name will be used in the document properties, templates and w record changes made to documents.
2. License Agreement	
3. User name	
4. Registration	First name — Anthony
	Last name — Price
	Initials — AP

Figure 10.05

4 The final stage gives you a choice of registration options. If you choose the default 'Register now' your browser will be opened and you will be taken to the registration page at the Open Office site. The registration process is a straightforward form-filling exercise which will just a few minutes.

5 Regardless of the registration option which you choose, clicking **Finish** (when you have finished) will end the registration process and launch the application.

Customizing and configuring Open Office

There are literally hundreds of configurable options in Open Office and how you set things up will largely depend on how you and/or your users like to work. However, there are one or two options that you will need to set. The example which follows was done from inside the Open Office Writer component, though it could have been done from any of the other components in the suite.

Most of the settings that we are interested in are accessed through the **Tools > Options** menu at the top of the Open Office screen. Clicking on **Options** will show a list of configurable elements (Figure 10.06).

This is a familiar Explorer type interface where clicking on a '+' sign will open up a list with further '+' signs to access sublists. Details are shown in the pane to the right.

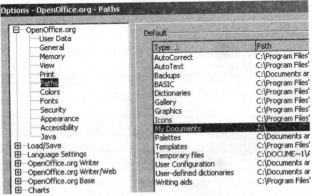

Figure 10.06

Setting paths to files

From the point of view of a networked office, one of the important groups of settings is the one that covers the paths to the shared file store and the location of document templates. To look at or change the path settings, navigate through the list structure until you see something like Figure 10.06.

In this example, Open Office was installed on to a PC which had the user's *My Documents* folder on a shared file store elsewhere on the network. This folder has been allocated the drive letter Z: in Windows, and the Open Office installer detected this and set it up as the default location for saving files.

Another path which you may want to modify is to the document template folder. If you look again at the figure you will see that the *Templates* folder is on the local C: drive. This contains the various standard Open Office templates for documents, etc. and if you create your own templates, by default they would also be stored here. A better solution is to create a separate *Templates* folder on a shared network drive and store user-defined templates there. If you had (say) a fax cover sheet with company logo or a blank presentation page they, and other templates, could be placed in a shared *Templates* folder so that everyone had access to them. To do this you need to create a new folder in Windows on a shared drive. If you can't remember how to do this, have another look at Chapter 2, *Sharing resources* or section 8.6, *Mapping a network drive* on page 124.

In this example, there is a folder on a shared network drive which has been allocated the drive letter Y: and all users have permission to use it. To make custom templates available to all users, we add the *Templates* folder to the Open Office search path.

1   Navigate to **Tools > Options > Paths** and highlight the **Templates** entry in the list.

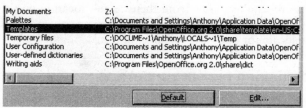

Figure 10.07

2 Click **Edit**. This will show the existing paths.

Figure 10.08

3 Click **Add**.

4 Navigate through the structure until you reach the *Templates* folder where you will keep your shared document templates.

Figure 10.09

5 Click **OK**. The system will confirm that the new folder has been added to the Open Office search path.

6 Click **OK** to accept the new settings and exit.

Note, that you have *added* a folder which will be used to store your user-defined shared templates. The default Open Office templates remain available from their default location on the local C: drive. The procedures outlined above can, of course, be used to relocate (or add) any folder on any available path.

Configuring file saving options

Like most software applications, Open Office has its own native file formats for saving documents. By default, Open Office will save files in these formats, using its own default *file extensions* which will identify the file types to the Windows Operating System. If necessary this can be changed.

How file extensions work

The name of a file on a Windows system consists of two parts: the name that the user gives it when it is created and a file extension which identifies the *file type* to the Operating System. If, for example, you create a file called *myfile* using the Microsoft Word word processor, Windows adds the extension .doc to the name and saves it as *myfile.doc.* This means that when you come to open that file again later, the .doc extension to the name, tells Windows to open the file with the Word package with which it was created. Other software packages have their own file extensions associated with them by default – *.xls* for Excel files, *.txt* for plain text files, and so on. These default values can be changed. For example, in the course of installing Open Office – step 7 – we chose to associate the file extensions normally associated with Microsoft's Word, Excel and PowerPoint packages with their Open Office equivalents instead.

Changing default save options

By default, Open Office saves the files you create, using its own file formats and extensions. For example, word processor files are normally saved with the extension *.odt* indicating that the file is in Open Document Text format. This extension is associated with the Open Office Writer package, so clicking on *myfile.odt* will tell Windows to open it with that application. However, if you handle a lot of (say) Word documents and have set up Open Office to open them instead of using Word (which you may not even have installed on your system) it can be inconvenient to save them in the default *.odt* format particularly if you regularly exchange files with Word users.

To change the default file format – and extension – when saving files:

1 Navigate to **Tools > Options** and select **General** from the **Load/Save** entry in the list.

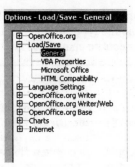

Figure 10.10

2 This presents you with the Load/Save options in two drop-down lists. Figure 10.11 shows the Open Office default association for text documents – to save in OpenDocument format. To change the default, scroll down the list on the right, select the new default format and click **OK**.

Figure 10.11

Use the drop-down list on the left to select any of the supported file types and the list on the right to change the default save option. For example, to change the way in which you save Open Office spreadsheets, select **Spreadsheet** from the drop-down list on the left and select **Microsoft Excel 97/2000/XP** from the list on the right. Click **OK** to make the change permanent.

Figure 10.12

If you have followed the suggestions in this chapter, you will be able to use the Open Office suite to open, modify and save word processor and spreadsheet files in Microsoft compatible file formats, and to share them with Microsoft users even if you don't have the Microsoft packages installed on your system.

10.3 How to install a web browser

All releases of the Windows operating system are shipped with a built-in web browser called Internet Explorer. This is the default browser for both XP and Vista. Many users have expressed concerns about the security of Internet Explorer, whilst others merely want to look at available (free) alternatives. Of these, the *Firefox* browser from the Mozilla project is one of the best known and most popular.

Downloading Firefox

Point your existing browser at:

http://www.mozilla.com/

and click on the **Download Firefox** button. Even on a 512Kbps connection the download is only a couple of minutes' work.

Installing Firefox

1   Click on the Firefox installer icon. You will be presented with a Welcome screen – click **Next** – followed by a License Agreement screen – accept and click **Next**.

2   Choose the Standard installation and click **Next**, then **Next** again. This will start the main installation process and Firefox will display a progress report. When the installer has finished the default action is to launch the Firefox browser.

3   Click **Finish** to exit the installer and launch the application.

When the newly-installed browser launches you may have to allow it through your firewall. Once done, Firefox will take you to the Updated page at the Mozilla site to confirm that you are running the latest version. Whenever Firefox updates itself there will be a one-off visit to the Updated page.

Configuring Firefox

With your new browser installed, you will probably want to change some of the settings. In particular, you will probably want to use your Favorites or Bookmarks from the browser which you have been using previously.

To import your bookmarks from a previous browser:

1 Start the Firefox browser.

2 Click on the **Bookmarks** menu and select **Manage Bookmarks**.

Figure 10.13

This will open the Bookmarks Management window.

3 Click on the **File** menu, then select **Import**. This will show you the options for importing bookmarks from other popular browsers or from a file.

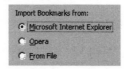

Figure 10.14

If your previous browser is one of the ones listed, all you have to do is select it and click **Next**. Its bookmarks will be imported. Click **Finish** when you are done.

If your previous browser is not listed, close Firefox and open your old browser. Somewhere in it you will find an Export Bookmarks (or similar) option. Select this and export your bookmarks – usually in HTML format – to a shared drive or floppy. Restart Firefox and choose the option to import from a file.

Changing other settings

Most settings in Firefox are set through the **Tools > Options** menu. Clicking on this menu item will bring up the Windows shown in Figure 10.15.

Most default settings for Firefox are suitable for most users, so there is little to do before you can use the browser. However, if you do want to change anything, like setting a new home page or modifying your privacy settings, or selecting a different area for downloaded files, this is the place to do it.

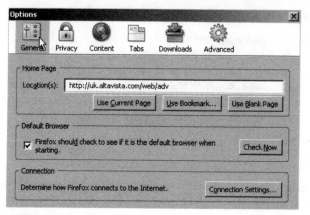

Figure 10.15

The Opera browser

This is yet another first-rate free alternative web browser. It can be downloaded from:

http://www.opera.com/download/

Just visit the site and click on the Download link. After the download completes, click on the installer icon and follow the instructions on screen. The makers of Opera call it the Fastest Browser on Earth and many users would agree with this. The current version of Opera (9) – has a built-in e-mail client and supports the downloading of bit torrent files through the browser – well worth a look.

10.4 Installing an e-mail client

Although there are differences of detail between e-mail clients there are very substantial similarities. They need to be installed and configured with user details, server addresses and passwords. In this example, we will be looking at the *Thunderbird* free e-mail client from Mozilla – makers of Firefox – though most of the material will apply in general terms to other e-mail programs, from the built-in client in Opera, to standalone programs such as *Iscribe* or *Kaufman Mail Warrior*.

Downloading and installing Thunderbird

Go to the Mozilla site and click on the **Thunderbird E-mail** link. This will direct you to the Thunderbird page. Click on the download link. On a 512Kbps connection it will take under two minutes to come in. Once the file is downloaded, click the icon to start the installer. This is almost identical to that of Firefox.

1 Click the icon to start the installer. Thunderbird unpacks it-self, and then displays a Welcome screen.

2 Click on **Next**. This takes you to the licence agreement.

3 Accept the licence terms, then click **Next** to continue. At the next screen you will be given a choice of a Standard or a Custom install. Select Standard, and click **Next** to start.

4 When the installer has finished, click **Finish** and launch the Thunderbird program.

Configuring Thunderbird

When Thunderbird starts for the first time it runs a setup wiz-ard. Make sure that you have user names, passwords and server addresses to hand so that you can provide them when prompted.

1 Start Thunderbird. You may be offered the opportunity to import settings from another mail client – do this if it suits you, but for this example, we will set up from scratch. The first screen that the setup program displays is the choice of what type of account you wish to use.

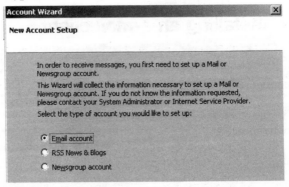

Figure 10.16

2 Accept the default, which is to set up an e-mail account. Click **Next**. You will then be presented with a dialog box where you enter your name (the one that will be seen by people receiving e-mail from the account) and the user name required by the mail system. Type them in and click **Next**.

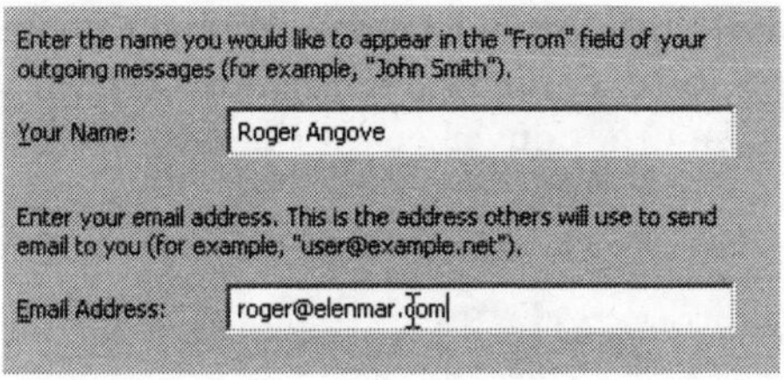

Enter the name you would like to appear in the "From" field of your outgoing messages (for example, "John Smith").

Your Name: Roger Angove

Enter your email address. This is the address others will use to send email to you (for example, "user@example.net").

Email Address: roger@elenmar.com

Figure 10.17

3 Select the mail type (in this case Post Office Protocol – POP) and enter the addresses for your incoming (POP) and outgoing (SMTP) servers. Click **Next** to continue.

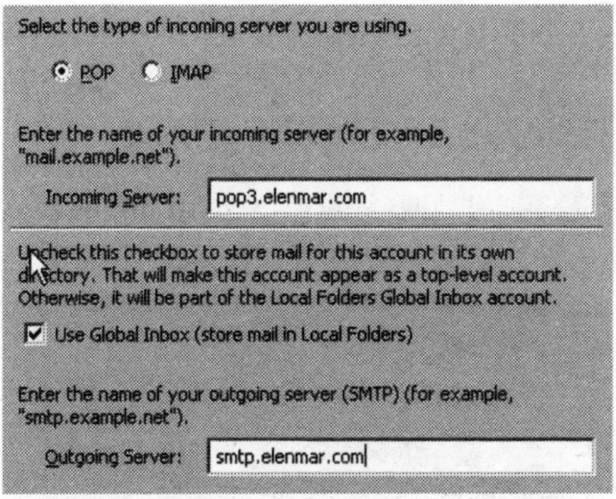

Select the type of incoming server you are using.

● POP ○ IMAP

Enter the name of your incoming server (for example, "mail.example.net").

Incoming Server: pop3.elenmar.com

Uncheck this checkbox to store mail for this account in its own directory. That will make this account appear as a top-level account. Otherwise, it will be part of the Local Folders Global Inbox account.

☑ Use Global Inbox (store mail in Local Folders)

Enter the name of your outgoing server (SMTP) (for example, "smtp.example.net").

Outgoing Server: smtp.elenmar.com

Figure 10.18 Note that the default is to store mail locally.

4 Enter the user name allocated by the mail system (typically your ISP). Most systems don't include the *@whatever* part of the address, but check your documentation just in case.

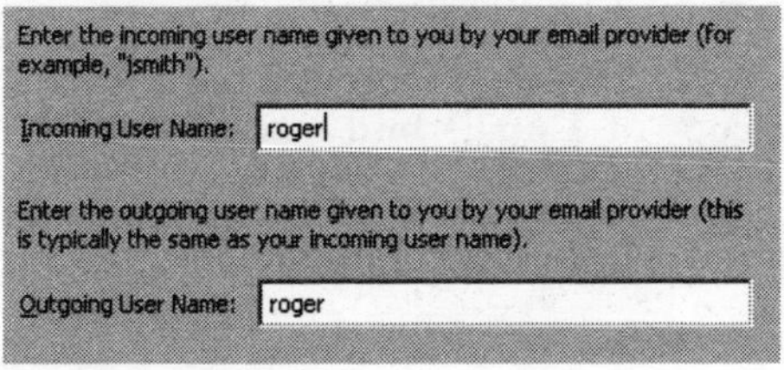

Enter the incoming user name given to you by your email provider (for example, "jsmith").

Incoming User Name: roger

Enter the outgoing user name given to you by your email provider (this is typically the same as your incoming user name).

Outgoing User Name: roger

Figure 10.19

Another point to note is that user names and details are usually the same for incoming and outgoing mail servers but this is not necessarily the case – again, check your documentation. Click **Next** when you are done.

5 The next screen shows the default name for the account based on the information that you have entered previously. This is simply the local name on the mail client, which may be changed to suit the convenience or taste of the user. You may change it to something more descriptive if you wish.

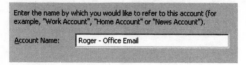

Figure 10.20

Click **Next** to continue.

6 The final stage of the setup process shows a summary of the information that you have entered. Check the information for accuracy. If you are going to use a shared file store machine on your network for storing the mail folders *uncheck* the **Download messages now** box, then click on **Finish**.

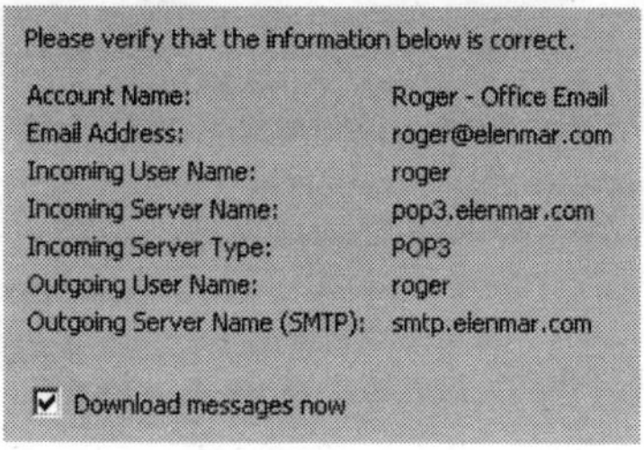

> Please verify that the information below is correct.
>
> Account Name: Roger - Office Email
> Email Address: roger@elenmar.com
> Incoming User Name: roger
> Incoming Server Name: pop3.elenmar.com
> Incoming Server Type: POP3
> Outgoing User Name: roger
> Outgoing Server Name (SMTP): smtp.elenmar.com
>
> ☑ Download messages now

Figure 10.21

Changing your e-mail settings

All of the settings which you entered can be changed from inside a running copy of Thunderbird – Server addresses, passwords, storage locations, etc.

To access the Thunderbird settings:

1 Start the application.

2 Highlight the **Local Folders** entry.

3 Select **Properties**.

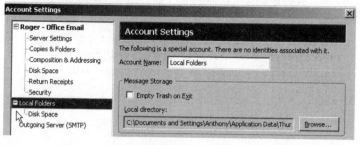

Figure 10.22

As you can see from Figure 10.22, all the Thunderbird settings – server addresses, etc. – can be edited here. Most of these are fairly straightforward and you can easily explore them for yourself. The only one that we will examine here is the process of relocating the default mail store.

Relocating the mail store

If you are using a shared file store on your network, it makes sense to store mail folders in a single location if only for the convenience of making backups. You can store your mail files on any drive which can be accessed over your LAN. This may be a mail folder for the user which is set up as a subfolder of the user's *My Documents* or a shared mail folder which contains a sub-folder for each user.

To create a mail folder on the shared file store for the user Roger:

1 Navigate to a shared drive (in this example Y:) in Windows and create a shared folder **ThunderbirdMail**.

2 Create a subfolder **Roger**.

3 Start the Thunderbird application.

4 Navigate to **Local Folders > Properties** as shown in the previous section, and click **Browse**. Navigate to the folder you created in Windows then click **OK**. Thunderbird will confirm the new mail store location. Roger's mail folders will now be included in the backups for your network.

10.5 Creating new accounts

To create a new user account you need to start the New Account Setup Wizard that you used when first installing Thunderbird. There are two ways of doing this.

1 Start Thunderbird.

2 Click on **Local Folders.**

3 Right-click and select properties, then click **Add Account.**

Or

4 Click the **Create a new account** icon in the pane on the right.

Figure 10.23

Either way, step through the Wizard and set up the new account along the lines described earlier in the chapter.

Summary

In this chapter we have looked at how to set up the free Open Office suite on your network to act as a seamless substitute for the Microsoft equivalent, including file sharing and compatibility with Microsoft users.

We have looked at two highly regarded (free) web browsers and how to set up the (free) Thunderbird e-mail client and integrate it with your backup system. Obviously no two businesses are the same and neither are their software needs. However, the material presented in this chapter will apply to most small businesses and may provide a basis for a standard software build which is one of the topics considered in Chapter 11, *Building a node*.

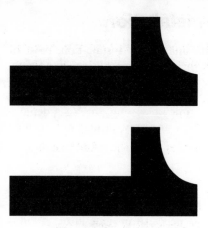

11

building a node

In this chapter you will learn:

- how to automate Windows installation (XP Professional)

- how to save a system image (Vista)

- the advantages of a standardized hardware platform

- how to clone and deploy a system image (XP Professional)

11.1 Unattended installation

There are several variants on unattended installation, most of which are intended for use in large corporate environments. However, Windows XP has one quite straightforward installation method using the standard installation CD and an 'answer file' on a floppy disk. (At the time of writing, the Vista deployment tools are still to be finalized and may, or may not, include something similar.)

Installing from CD

As you saw in Chapter 8, *Installing Windows*, the person who is installing the operating system needs to provide information – product key, language settings, administrator password and so forth – from time to time as the installation proceeds. This is time-consuming. You will waste a lot of time watching progress bars crawl across the display, waiting for the next prompt. However, the installation process can be automated by putting the necessary information in a text file on a removable disk. To do this, you will need your Windows installation CD and a formatted blank floppy disk.

Creating an answer file

1 Put the Windows installation CD in the CD-ROM drive. Hold down [Shift] when you do this to stop it from autoplaying.

2 Click on the **My Computer** icon on your Desktop and navigate to the drive which has the installation CD in it.

A note on OEM versions of Windows

If you have an Original Equipment Manufacturer version of Windows you have no choice but to use the 'Restore' disks provided to carry out an installation over which you have little control. If you happen to find the manufacturer's default settings and installed applications convenient, fine. Otherwise you will have to do a certain amount of post-install tweaking. The contents of this chapter only apply to standard versions of Windows.

---

3 Right-click and select **Explore**.

4 Navigate to the \SUPPORT\TOOLS folder.

Figure 11.01

5 This folder contains a file called DEPLOY.CAB. Click on the file name to open DEPLOY.CAB and list its contents.

cvtarea.exe   deploy.chm   factory.exe   oformat.com

setupmgr.exe   sysprep.exe   setupcl.exe   ref.chm

Figure 11.02

6 Click on SETUPMGR.EXE to start the Setup Manager Wizard. You will see a standard Welcome screen. Click **Next**. You will be presented with a choice to modify an existing file or to create a new one. Choose the new file option and click **Next** to continue.

7 At the next screen you will be asked to choose the type of answer file that you want to make. In this case, accept the default – unattended setup – and click **Next** to continue.

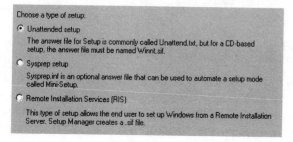

Choose a type of setup:

⦿ Unattended setup

The answer file for Setup is commonly called Unattend.txt, but for a CD-based setup, the answer file must be named Winnt.sif.

○ Sysprep setup

Sysprep.inf is an optional answer file that can be used to automate a setup mode called Mini-Setup.

○ Remote Installation Services (RIS)

This type of setup allows the end user to set up Windows from a Remote Installation Server. Setup Manager creates a .sif file.

Figure 11.03

8 At the next screen, select the Windows version that you are using – Windows is pretty good at detecting this so it's just a case of checking and accepting the default. Click **Next**.

9 At the next screen, choose the **Fully Automated** option, then click **Next** to continue.

10 At the next screen choose **Set up from a CD**. Click **Next**.

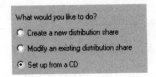

Figure 11.04

11 The next screen is the Licence agreement. Check the box, then click **Next** to accept it.

With the licence terms accepted, Setup Manager now takes you through a form-filling process in which you enter the information that you would otherwise enter interactively in the course of a standard install. Progress is reported in the pane on the left of the window. Obviously the values that you supply in this extended dialog box will depend on your setup. Much of the time you will be able to use Windows defaults settings, though you will of course have to supply specifics such as your workgroup name, etc.

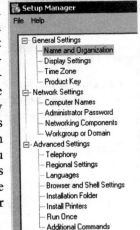

Figure 11.05

12 When prompted you need to provide a valid **Product Key** – be especially careful with this. Setup Manager will allow you to put in an invalid key at this point and you will only discover this when, later, your installation fails.

13 Another trap for the unwary is at the **Computer Names** part. If you give the PC a name at this point (which is the default) and you then use your unattended install disk to build more

than one node you will end up with duplicate names on your network and this will cause you problems. At this point, then, choose the option to **Automatically generate** names. (You can always rename your nodes(s) later.)

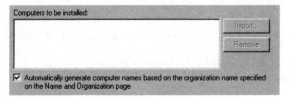

Figure 11.06

14 At the **Administrator password** dialog box, select the **Encrypt** option – *not* the Automatic logon option. These are basic security precautions. Automatic logons are always poor security practice in a workplace, and storing an unencrypted password in a text file on a floppy disk is asking for trouble.

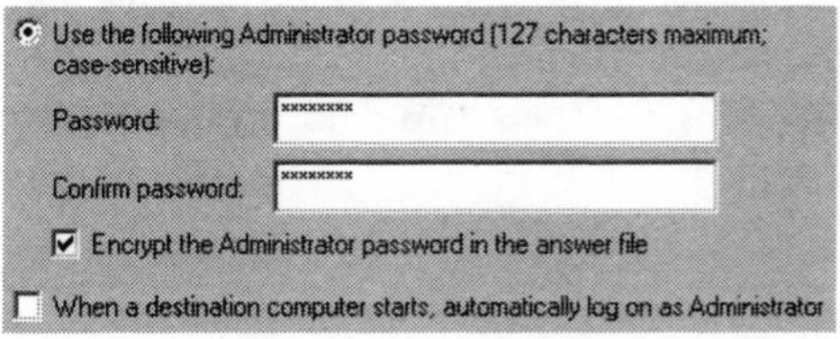

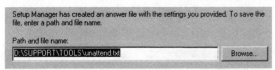

Figure 11.07

15 Step through the remainder of the Setup Manager process, entering the values appropriate to your organization. At the end you will be prompted to save your answer file.

Setup Manager has created an answer file with the settings you provided. To save the file, enter a path and file name.

Path and file name:

D:\SUPPORT\TOOLS\unattend.txt   Browse...

Figure 11.08

By default you will be supplied with both a file name and a path. *You need to change both of these*. Put a blank, formatted floppy disk in the A: drive, then use **Browse** to set a path to it. When you have done this, change the file extension. Instead of saving the file as *unattend.txt* save it is *winnt.sif*. When you have renamed the file click **Save**.

11.2 Unattended installations

After you have made your answer file and saved it to a floppy, you can use it and your Windows installation CD to build as many workstation nodes as you wish. All that is required is that the PC will boot to the CD-ROM drive and that it has a floppy drive. If you don't have a built-in floppy drive, you may be able to use an external USB floppy or a pen drive for your answer file, though you may need to edit path details in the batch file on the removable drive.

If your target PC is not set to boot from the CD-ROM drive as its first option, you must use the CMOS/BIOS setup utility to do this. If you have forgotten how to do this, turn back to *Checking CMOS/BIOS settings* (page 111) before you begin.

Starting the install

1   Put the Windows installation CD in the drive and the floppy disk in the floppy drive and restart the PC. Note – the floppy disk is used to store the setup data files and should *not* be a bootable or startup disk.

2   As the PC reboots, you will see a message to 'Press any Key' to initiate the boot to CD-ROM. If you miss this, the system will boot, or attempt to boot to the previously installed Windows version that is already on the hard drive. Obviously, this isn't a problem where you are installing to a new disk.

3   The Windows installer will run for a few minutes until you are prompted for partitioning information. The installer will show the existing partition scheme and, by default, will suggest installing to the current Windows partition.

```
C:   Partition1 [NTFS]                          8182  MB
     Unpartitioned space                           8  MB
```

Figure 11.09

Your best bet at this point is to exercise the option to delete the existing partition and reformat it with the NTFS file system. This will take slightly longer than the alternative which is to install to the existing partition by deleting the existing Windows installation or overwriting it. The advantage of doing a full reformat of the disk (*not* the quick format option) is that you are starting from scratch and any errors in the file system will be erased. Make your choice – follow the on-screen instructions (choose the NTFS file system) and the file system format will begin. When it has finished, the installer will start to copy files to the hard disk. No further input will be required from you until it has finished. This may be anywhere between half an hour and an hour depending on the speed of your system.

Finishing the install

Windows picks up the standard installation at the point where it prompts you to adjust the screen resolution, then runs through the Automatic Updates options before taking you to the Welcome screen and inviting you to 'Spend a few minutes setting up your computer'. From this point on the procedures are the same as for the standard interactive install described in Chapter 8.

Finally, don't forget to remove the installation CD and the floppy disk from their respective drives and put them somewhere safe.

11.3 Saving a system image (Vista)

This consists of making a snapshot of the complete installation – operating system, applications, shortcuts, the lot. The technique is possible in XP or the Home editions of Vista if you use third-party tools such as *Norton Ghost* or *Acronis True Image* but the capability for drive imaging is built into the Professional versions of Vista, and we will look at its tools for doing this.

(Although the details of third-party tools on other operating systems will be different, the underlying concepts are similar, so working though this section can still be a useful thing to do.)

Backing up

1 Navigate to **Start > Control Panel** and select the **Back up your computer** option from **System and Maintenance**.

System and Maintenance
Get started with Windows
Back up your computer

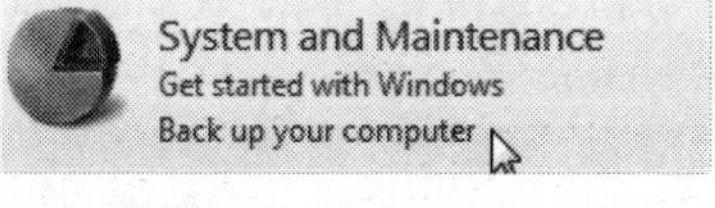

Figure 11.10

2 Choose the 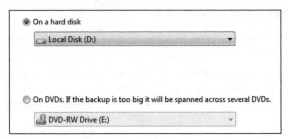 option.

3 You will now be given a choice of where to backup – either a locally attached disk drive (including USB attached drives) or burning to DVD. In this instance the choice is between a locally attached hard disk (which *must* be formatted with the NTFS file system) or burning to DVD. We will back up to the hard disk, though the procedures for backing up to DVD are essentially similar.

Figure 11.11

4 Having chosen your target drive for the backup (in this case D:) click **Next**. Vista will confirm your choices of source and destination drives – we are going to backup C: to D: – so having checked this, click **Start Backup**. Vista will start the backup procedure and output a progress report as it works. This will probably take several minutes. When the process is finished, click **Close**.

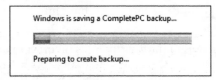

Figure 11.12

5 At this point you may like to check for yourself that the backup file is where it should be. If you navigate to the backup drive (D: in this case) Vista will show a folder with the name **WindowsImageBackup** and the date that the backup was done. This folder will be your source when you come to re-store your system.

Restoring

The restore process requires you to attach the source drive (or have the DVD disk to hand) and boot to the Vista installation DVD. Thus restoring from DVD requires *two* drives – one for the boot DVD and one for the image file you want to restore. In this example, we will restore from an attached hard disk.

Note: the restore process repartitions the operating system disk and *destroys everything on it* before restoring your saved image. With this in mind we will begin.

1 Put the Vista installation DVD in the drive – change the boot order in CMOS if necessary – and restart the PC.

2 When prompted, Press any key to boot to the installation CD and start the Vista installer. Allow it to run until you see the screen where you set the language and keyboard layout.

3 Set the language and keyboard layout, then click **Next**.

4 Click on **System Recovery Options**.

5 Select a keyboard layout (again) and click **Next**. The recovery system will now spend some time probing your system before giving you a menu of recovery options.

6 From the recovery options, click **Complete PC Restore**.

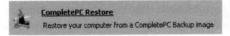

Figure 11.13

7 This launches the (rather dramatically named) Windows Disaster Recovery Wizard which will list available sources – in this case, drive D: with the date and time stamp of the backup that we made earlier.

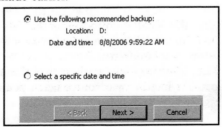

Figure 11.14

8 Select the backup image and click **Next** to start the recovery process.

9 At the next screen accept the default suggestion to format and repartition all disks (unless you have a local data partition on the disk, and you should not have on a network node) then click **Finish**. You will then receive a final warning about all the existing information being destroyed.

10 Check the box to confirm that you want to delete everything, then click **OK** to proceed. The recovery process will take a while – at least as long as the initial backup. When it is complete, remove the DVD from the drive and power down. Detach the D: drive which you used as the source for the recovery operation and reboot the PC.

You should now be looking at an installation of Vista which is identical to the one you saved.

Limitations of the Vista image/restore

Saving an image of a drive and subsequently restoring it is obviously a useful technique. It is not confined to Vista, indeed it has been in use with earlier Windows versions through third-party disk imaging software for several years. However, it is essentially a one-to-one backup method: for each drive there is a corresponding saved image. Clearly there are advantages in having a one-to-many system where a single image can be saved and restored to any number of target systems. However, there are two problems which need to be overcome in order to do this, hardware limitations and operating system security.

Hardware limitations

When you install a copy of Windows on to a system, the installer configures the installation to run on that particular set of hardware. If you then make an image of your installation and attempt to restore it to a different hardware setup it will, in all probability, fail. Some components – typically things fitted in expansion slots, like internal modems or network cards – can be quite forgiving, but if the hard disk controllers or BIOS chips are different you will have problems, to say the least. It pays, then, to have the smallest possible number of hardware builds on your network. It makes management and deployment much easier, reduces down-time of your network nodes and generally reduces long-term operational costs.

11.4 Windows security

With earlier versions of Windows it was possible to clone a drive – that is, to make an image of an installation – and to restore it onto a different PC with a similar hardware configuration. This rapidly became a means of stealing copies of Windows: all you needed to do was to buy a single licensed copy, make a disk image and clone it across as many compatible systems as you wanted. There were, of course, legitimate uses for cloning, and it is still used by the volume system builders and by corporations rolling out large fleets of identical, or near identical, PCs. However, to make theft by copying more difficult, Microsoft added some extra security features to the modern editions of Windows. They also provided some tools to make legitimate disk imaging possible.

Cloning a Windows installation

To do this you will need:

* Compatible – preferably identical – hardware
* Third-party imaging software such as *Ghost* or *True Image*
* The Windows deployment tools.

As noted earlier in the chapter, the Vista deployment tools have not been finalized at the time of writing. The final release will almost certainly ship with a Vista version of SYSPREP.EXE which is the main tool used to prepare a Windows installation for duplication. However, the example used in this chapter is based on XP Professional, and there may be differences of detail when working with other Windows releases. As always, check the documentation of *your* system before starting work.

Windows security identifiers

When you install Windows on a PC it creates a Security Identifier (SID) which uniquely identifies that installation on that machine. This is an entirely behind-the-scenes operation which you might never notice until you try to image a drive without taking it into account. If you were to make an image of a Windows installation on one PC and restore it on another, you would meet problems when you attempted to network them because you would have two machines with the same SID. The deployment tools – specifically SYSPREP.EXE – offer a solution to this.

In outline, the cloning process works like this:

1 Create a master copy of the installation on the source PC by installing and configuring Windows and the applications – office suite, browser, etc. – that you want to include in your standard-build image.

2 Use SYSPREP.EXE to remove SIDs on the source machine.

3 Create as many images as you need of the stripped down installation.

4 Restore the cloned image to another (hardware compatible) PC and allow Windows to create a new SID, unique to that installation, when it first starts up.

Creating the master copy

1 Start with a clean install of Windows, either a standard one or an unattended install from an answer file. *Do not* join a domain during this initial installation even if you intend to join one later.

2 Log on using the Administrator account and install and configure any applications that you want to be part of your standard software build.

Installing the deployment tools

1 Create a folder on the system partition of the source PC and give it the name *\Sysprep*. For most of us the partition will be the C: drive so the location of the folder will be *C:\Sysprep*. (Note: capitalization of the name is not important, but its name and location are. When a Sysprepped Windows installation boots for the first time, it automatically removes the *\Sysprep* folder and its contents to prevent accidental damage by a user idly clicking on it.)

2 Put the Windows installation CD in the drive and navigate to \SUPPORT\TOOLS.

3 Click on the DEPLOY.CAB file to show its contents.

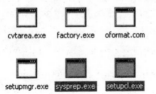

cvtarea.exe   factory.exe   oformat.com

setupmgr.exe   sysprep.exe   setupcl.exe

Figure 11.15

4 Copy the files SYSPREP.EXE and SETUPCL.EXE to the \Sysprep folder that you created on the PC's hard disk.

5 Navigate to your \Sysprep folder (if you're not already there) and click on the SYSPREP.EXE icon to run the program. You will be shown a summary of what the Sysprep tool does.

6 Read the text and, if the licence terms apply to you, click on the **OK** button to continue. You will now be presented with some choices about how to run Sysprep. Choose the options to **Shut down** and **Reseal** as indicated in Figure 11.16.

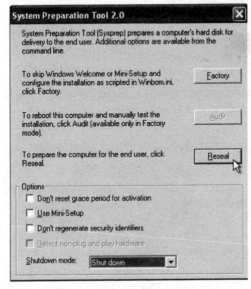

Figure 11.16

7 Click **Reseal,** and you will see a notice which summarizes your choices.

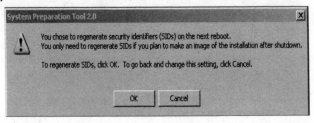

Figure 11.17

8 Removing Security Identifiers (SIDs) to be regenerated on the next boot is *exactly* what you want to do. Click **OK.** Sysprep will work in the background for half a minute or so, and then the system will shut down. *Do not* restart the master system until you have cloned the drive.

Creating the disk image

The details of how you create the disk image will depend on what disk-cloning software you use for the job. In outline, the process is:

1 Run the System preparation utility to remove SIDs on the Master or source PC.

2 Close down the system.

3 Save the contents of the prepared drive to a single file on a separate drive.

Saving an image – a worked example

The example that follows clones the C: drive of the source system to an attached D: drive which has been formatted with the NTFS file system. The C: drive has been prepared for duplication with SYSPREPEXE as described earlier. The software used is *Acronis True Image* – other disk-duplicating software will be broadly similar in its operation.

1 Boot to the Acronis CD and choose the **full version** option from the menu. This will take you to a screen of options.

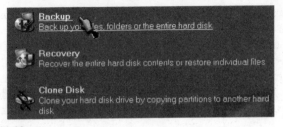

Figure 11.18

2 Choose the **Backup** option (*not* **Clone Disk**) and click to launch the Create Backup Wizard.

3 Click **Next** on the Wizard's opening screen and choose the default **Entire disk** option.

4 Click **Next**. The imaging software will spend a few seconds analysing your system before presenting you with a report.

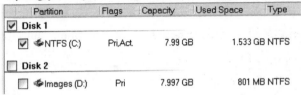

	Partition	Flags	Capacity	Used Space	Type
☑	**Disk 1**				
☑	NTFS (C:)	Pri,Act.	7.99 GB	1.533 GB NTFS	
☐	**Disk 2**				
☐	Images (D:)	Pri	7.997 GB	801 MB NTFS	

Figure 11.19

5 Here we have two hard disks and the software has defaulted to backing up C: to the attached D: drive, which is what we want to do. Click **Next**. Ignore any message about differential or incremental backups.

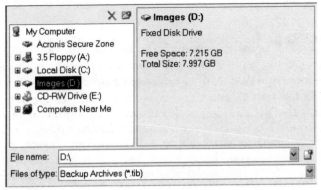

Figure 11.20

6 You will be given a choice of locations for your backup file. As you can see from the figure, this imaging software gives the option to store the image file on a local disk, a CD/DVD drive, or across the network. In this example, we will back up to the D: drive, though the basic procedure would be the same irrespective of the target. Having chosen the D: drive as the target, give the target file a meaningful name. Click **Next**.

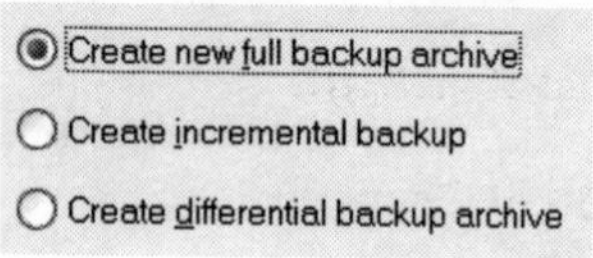

> ◉ Create new full backup archive
>
> ○ Create incremental backup
>
> ○ Create differential backup archive

Figure 11.21

7 Choose **Create new full backup archive**, and click **Next**. You will be given some further options. You may want to put a password on your image file, or to change the default level of compression. Explore the options and make your choices.

8 Click **Next**. You will now be given the opportunity to add some comments to accompany your image file. Add your comments, then click **Next** to continue. The imaging software will now summarize your choices of file name, paths, comments, etc.

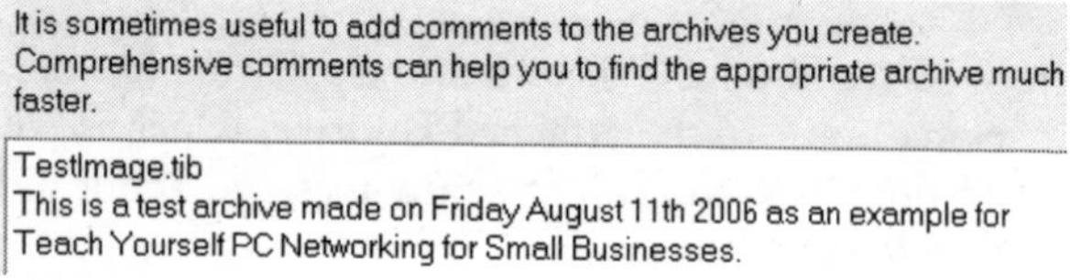

> It is sometimes useful to add comments to the archives you create.
> Comprehensive comments can help you to find the appropriate archive much faster.

> TestImage.tib
> This is a test archive made on Friday August 11th 2006 as an example for Teach Yourself PC Networking for Small Businesses.

Figure 11.22

9 Click **Proceed** to continue. The imaging software will now make the required image and output a progress report as it does so. At the end of the imaging process you will see a completion message.

10 Click **OK** to finish.

Having saved an image file to a disk, you can now copy it as many times as you like, or simply use it as a master copy from which you can restore any number of times. Because you used the Sysprep utility to prepare your disk before imaging, every time it is restored, Windows will run its mini set-up routine on first boot and create new (and unique) Security Identifiers for the newly installed system. Providing you are using a standard hardware build for your nodes, you can rebuild any number of nodes any number of times from a single image. Obviously, the fewer different hardware types there are on your network, the smaller the number of images are needed to maintain it.

Deploying the disk image

This is a three-stage process:

1   Connect to the storage medium where you stored the disk image.

2   Restore the image using your imaging software.

3   Reboot the restored image and go through the abbreviated Windows Set up routine.

Restoring an image – a worked example

In this example it is assumed that you have fitted a new hard drive to one of your systems to replace one that has failed. The drive has been fitted, but not partitioned or formatted. Your task is to restore a working installation of Windows from an image file that you created earlier.

1   Physically install the new hard disk. Because it has no partition and is unformatted it will not be allocated a drive letter.

2   Boot the PC to your imaging software. Step through the opening screens as before until you reach the menu to choose between backup and restore operations. Choose **Recovery** (to restore from a saved image).

3   Step through the various pages and options presented by the Wizard until you reach the screen to select your archive (Figure 11.23).

    In this example we will be restoring from an image on the C: drive. However, the image file could equally well be mounted with a different drive letter or from a network share – hence the importance of the file name and the comments field.

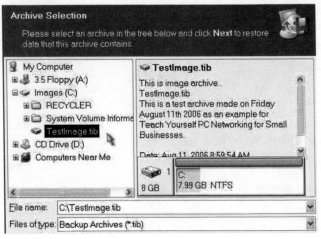

Figure 11.23

4 Select the appropriate image file, then click **Next**. This will take you to a screen where you can choose the restore type.

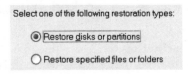

Figure 11.24

5 Choose **Restore disks or partitions,** and click **Next**.

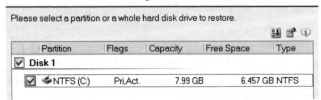

Figure 11.25

6 Tick the boxes to confirm that you want to restore NTFS C: then click **Next**.

7 Confirm that you want to restore to the unallocated space on Disk 1 – the new disk that you installed earlier. Click **Next**. Skip over the next screen (which gives the opportunity to restore from a different image) by clicking **Next** again.

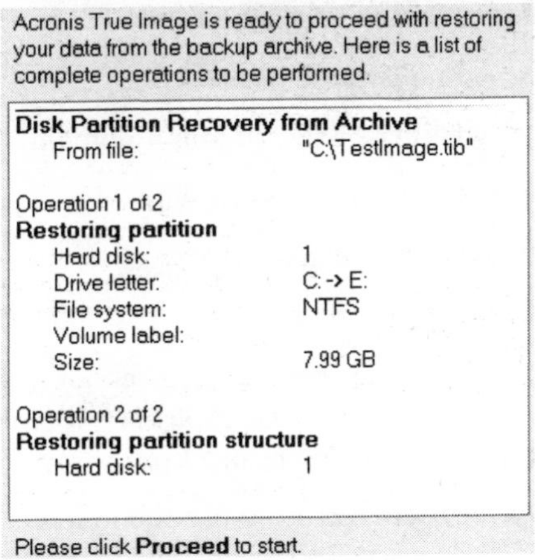

Acronis True Image is ready to proceed with restoring
your data from the backup archive. Here is a list of
complete operations to be performed.

Disk Partition Recovery from Archive
    From file: "C:\TestImage.tib"

Operation 1 of 2
Restoring partition
    Hard disk: 1
    Drive letter: C: → E:
    File system: NTFS
    Volume label:
    Size: 7.99 GB

Operation 2 of 2
Restoring partition structure
    Hard disk: 1

Please click **Proceed** to start.

Figure 11.26

The summary screen shows the operations that that the imaging
software will carry out when you click **Proceed**. You may notice
that the drive letters are not what you expected. Don't worry
about this – after the image has been restored to the disk and the
system has been rebooted to it, the proper drive letters will be
restored and the system will boot to (the new) C: as normal.

8 Click **Proceed**. The software will display the familiar progress
    report while it works and confirm completion when it is done.

9 Click **OK** and power down the PC.

Booting the restored image for the first time

1 Remove the imaging software from the CD drive.

2 Remove the disk containing the image file and store it some-
    where safe for future use.

3 Start the PC. Instead of booting directly to a working sys-
    tem, Windows will display the Welcome screen that you would
    normally meet towards the end of a conventional install.

4 From this point onwards proceed as for the last stages of a
    conventional install, clicking **Next** as necessary:

    ♦ Accept the licence agreement

    ♦ Choose your Automatic Updates options

- Allocate a name to the system
- Set the Administrator password
- Choose whether or not to join a domain
- Register (or not) the system with Microsoft
- Create user accounts(s)
- Finish.

5 For each user on that workstation: reboot and log in as that user and redirect their **My Documents** folder to point to their files on the shared file store machine.

You and/or your users can now use the system. The operation has restored Windows and all the installed applications that were part of your original software build in a fraction of the time that it would have taken if you had started from scratch: installing Windows, installing the applications one by one, and so on.

Summary

In this chapter we have looked at how to automate much of the process of installing Windows and how to create and restore an image of a complete installed system. We have seen how to use one-to-one images using the built-in tools in Vista and one-to-many images using proprietary imaging software, where a single image can be deployed across any number of hardware compatible systems. Some of the procedures may appear complex at first sight – in particular, the business of source and destination drives changing their drive letters can be confusing. However, the time and work savings that you will gain from learning these techniques will be amply repaid in obtaining very fast build times and reducing down-time for your users.

12 client/server networks

In this chapter you will learn:

- about client/server networks

- about hardware requirements and network operating systems

- how to install a workgroup server

- how to configure a gateway

- how to configure a domain controller

12.1 Client/server v peer networks

So far, we have considered only peer networks. We have looked at, and worked through, the process of sharing files and resources between peers in a Windows workgroup. We have built on this to create a shared file store in which all user files are stored on a single workgroup server to gain the advantages of centralized backup of data from a single PC. We have noted some of the security limitations of such an approach and the amount of work involved in managing multiple user accounts which are distributed across all network nodes. For many small businesses, the relative insecurity of a peer network is acceptable, as are the overheads involved in administering a decentralized system. However, as the network grows in size and/or complexity, the limitations of the peer network become more of a problem, and it may be time to consider setting up a client/server network where all user accounts are held on and managed from a *Domain Controller* – a dedicated server which is running a Network Operating System (NOS) – requiring all users to log in to the network in order to use network services.

Characteristics of network types

Peer network	Client/server network
Uses standard desktop Windows operating system throughout.	Uses Windows for the client nodes, but a dedicated NOS for the server.
Each user needs a user account on each PC that s/he uses.	Each user has a single user account and can log in from anywhere.
Each user account needs to be managed on each node of the network – folder permissions, access rights, etc. have to be set up and maintained on each PC where the user has an account.	User accounts and security are centrally managed on the server box. You can also set password complexity and renewal policies for additional security.
Setting up a new user account for a new employee requires work on both the desktop PC and the workgroup server.	New user accounts can be set up in minutes on the server and be available immediately on any networked workstation PC.
Requires no technical knowledge other than Windows basics.	Requires knowledge of the network operating system used.

If you are operating a small business with a relatively low staff turnover and your security needs to be good but not on a par with the military or the banking sector, a peer network with a workgroup server for file sharing, etc. will probably meet your needs. On the other hand, if you have more than (say) 10 users, or users come and go frequently so that user accounts have to be created and removed from the distributed system regularly, you may find it worthwhile to move to a client/server system. If you are concerned about security, the centralized client/server model imposes the requirement for any and every user to be authenticated against the domain controller, so casual unauthorized access to your system and data becomes impossible and the opportunities for expert hacking and cracking are greatly reduced. (There is no such thing, by the way, as a 100% secure system. See Chapter 14, *Security*.)

Network infrastructure

Whether you are using a peer network or a client/server system, the bulk of your physical infrastructure will be the same: cable types and runs; deployment of hubs/switches/routers; even the location of the patch panel and the server box remain the same. The main differences are the hardware needed to run the server and the network operating system needed to control the network. For a small network, the central server box need not be particularly powerful or sophisticated compared with its workgroup server counterpart on a peer network. The total number of client PCs, required response times and the software applications that you run are more important considerations when specifying your server hardware than the type of network you are setting up.

Server hardware requirements

There isn't a single simple answer to this. Some network operating systems are more demanding of resources than others and the number of users and the services that you provide to them will also enter into the calculation.

Microsoft Small Business Server 2003 comes with these recommendations from Microsoft, shown in Table 12.01.

Component	Light load	Medium load	Heavy load
CPU	PIII 500MHz	PII 600MHz	Xeon 2GHz
RAM	512MB	1GB	1.5GB
Hard disks	2 or more with 8GB available for Windows 2003 Server	3 – using hardware RAID with SATA or SCSI drives	5 or more – hardware RAID with SCSI drives
LAN adaptors	100/10Mbps	100/10Mbps	100/10Mbps

Table 12.01 Hardware requirements for Windows 2003 Server.

These requirements were put forward when 2003 Server was released and are not particularly demanding by today's standards. Obviously, more is better, but the requirements for Windows will be ample for other network operating systems. Note, too, the emphasis on RAID technology (look back to Chapter 7, *Fault tolerance and disaster recovery* for more on this) and be aware that Linux distributions also support software RAID. Software RAID is technically less efficient than its hardware counterpart, but it is free.

Services

At the risk of stating the obvious, a server machine exists to provide services. Unlike a member of a peer network, a server box exists *only* to provide services. It is not used as a workstation and should be physically secure – preferably in a locked room. The main services which your server can provide are:

- **Domain controller** – this is at the heart of the client/server relationship. A single machine controls access to user accounts, data and other services. Users are required to log in with a user name and password to access anything on the network.

- **File server** – all user files are stored on (what should be) a secure central file store which has a backup system which operates independently of the users.

- **Print server** – centralized control of print jobs.

- **Gateway** – you can use your server box as the gateway to the Internet. This requires two network cards: one connecting to the Internet and the other as part of your private LAN. The private address is then configured as the gateway address on your client PCs and their requests for web pages, etc. are routed through your server.

* **Firewall** – an extension of the gateway role. You can implement a firewall on your gateway machine.

* **DHCP server** – if you want to use the Dynamic Host Configuration Protocol to allocate IP addresses to your client PCs you can run your DHCP server from the main server box if you wish.

This list is not exhaustive. Most server systems will offer mail servers, remote access facilities, the possibility of running a web server and so on. However, most small businesses are probably better off implementing some (if not all) of the services listed and using external hosted services for e-mail and the website. Another point worth making is that, although the domain controller service is the defining service in a client/server network, other services, such as DHCP or gateway can be implemented through a server which is not configured as a domain controller. Linux and Linux-based systems, in particular, can provide all these services when set up as a workgroup server, though of course you don't have the advantages of the centralized control of user access and passwords that you would if you were using it as a domain controller.

12.2 Network operating systems

Unlike a peer network on a Windows workgroup, a client/server system needs a domain controller which is running a network operating system. There are a number of choices, and what you choose will depend on your computing needs as well as your budget. The main choices for the small business are:

* Windows

* Netware

* Linux

* SME 7 (based on CentOS Linux)

We will consider each of these in turn.

Windows

The main Microsoft network operating system for small business use is *Windows Small Business Server 2003*. This is a cut-down of the full *2003 Server* system and has some limitations compared with the full product. Most of these are acceptable for most small businesses: you can only run a single server and the maximum number of users is 50. Buying the product gives you five Client Access Licences (CALs) and if you want to have more than this, you will have to buy further CALs. Different arrangements and pricing options are available so a visit to the Microsoft site or a phone call to a software vendor is advisable.

The main advantages of Windows are its familiarity and the wide availability of third-party support services if you need them. If you can install Windows XP, then you are already familiar with much of what is required to install the server version. Its documentation is adequate to get you started and there are useful and authoritative books available from Microsoft Press. In terms of third-party technical support, Microsoft products are (for better or for worse) the mainstream, so finding a local company who have staff trained to support them is relatively easy.

The main disadvantages of Windows as a server are acquisition and licensing costs and hardware requirements. Because it uses a Graphical User Interface (GUI) for server management, Windows is fairly demanding, particularly in terms of RAM. Some people have also expressed reservations about its security. Whether – as some commentators claim – Windows is inherently less secure than its rivals is a matter on which I, for one, will reserve judgement. What is undeniable, however, is that as the most commonly used operating system in the world, it is a common target for malefactors.

The successor to 2003 Server – *Longhorn Server* – is currently under development as the Microsoft server platform for the Vista era. It seems probable that there will be a Small Business version of this, though it has not yet been officially announced.

Netware

Long before Microsoft moved into the server market with their NT products – the forerunners of 2003 Server – the LAN market was dominated by Novell's *Netware* system. It provides file, print and directory services in much the same way as its rivals. Novell offer special pricing deals for people who are migrating from rival systems, such as the various Windows servers.

Novell pioneered the development of the LAN in the early 1980s and were one of the first companies to introduce technical qualifications for engineers supporting their products. Consequently, it is relatively easy to find qualified local support for Novell products almost anywhere in the world. Product details and pricing are available from the Novell website, as are details of their support services and partners.

Linux

Linux was developed by Linus Torvalds while a student at the University of Helsinki in 1991. It started as a student project which he described as: 'just a hobby [that] won't be big and professional'. The aim was to produce a free Unix-like operating system as an alternative to commercial releases of Unix which would run on the same sorts of PCs that were dominated by Windows. The official Linux mascot – proposed by Linus and originally drawn by Larry Ewing – appears on most Linux products.

Thanks to the appeal of Tux, the penguin, not to mention the Internet, the ever-increasing power and decreasing cost of hardware and licensing that ensures that it is free and will remain free, Linux has grown from a small private project to the fastest developing operating system ever. Worldwide, there are tens of millions of Linux installations and it is particularly significant in the operation of the Internet. The chances are somewhat better then 50/50 that when you log in to a website it will be running on a Linux server.

As a network operating system, Linux can be used as a server for Windows – and other – networks. The key to this is running a SAMBA server which uses Server Message Blocks (SMBs) to communicate with Windows PCs. (It can also, by the way, run server software to network old versions of Novell Netware and older Apple Macs which still run the Appletalk protocol.) It is, however, principally a TCP/IP based system which is well suited to Windows networks and the Internet.

Linux distributions

The Linux operating system is free in the sense of being distributed without any licensing costs. It is also open source – that is, its source code is freely available to everyone. Unlike closed source software, where the source code is a closely guarded commercial secret, Linux code can be examined, modified and passed on by anyone who has the skills to do this. This has been another of the factors which have promoted its rapid growth. Thousands of programmers worldwide, examine, tweak and develop both the core operating system and its associated applications, and these developments are also released freely as open source.

Deploying Linux on your LAN

Although the Linux operating system is free, companies who gather together its component parts and associated applications (like the Linux version of Open Office) may charge for the costs of distribution media (CDs, DVDs, etc.), documentation such as manuals, and support services. There are a number of companies offering Linux distributions on this basis and if you are interested in using Linux as a server on your LAN, your best bet may be to buy disks, manuals (and possibly support services) from one of the major Linux companies. The big players are:

* Red Hat Linux – US-based, and the biggest Linux company
* SuSE Linux – originally German, now US-owned (by Novell)
* Mandriva Linux – French, Red Hat based system.

All of these companies offer commercial as well as free community releases of Linux. Providing you have the manuals and the patience to learn, you can install Linux on a server in around an hour. The next task is to install and configure a SAMBA server and set the server to act as a domain controller. These are non-trivial tasks and it may take you some time and a lot of experimentation to get it right, but you will end up with a rock solid secure network operating system at very little cost.

SME 7 (Linux based)

SME Server is a free small business server product available as a download from www.contribs.org. There is also a supported commercial version of SME from Mitel Networks who sponsor (but do not support) the free edition.

SME is based on CentOS Linux which is a free derivative of a commercial Linux distribution from 'a prominent North American Linux vendor', so it is largely compatible with Red Hat Linux.

The main strength of the SME system is, perhaps, that it delivers the reliability and security of Linux, but doesn't require any Linux knowledge to implement. Provided that you can read and follow the instructions, it can be installed in a few minutes, and day-to-day management is through a web-based *server–manager* interface. This interface can be accessed from any Windows (or other) PC on the network through any standard web browser such as Firefox by typing in the server's IP address in the form <your server's IP address>/*server-manager* and logging in to the 'admin' account on the server. There is also a text-based server console for some operations and you can, if you wish, use a Linux command line.

12.3 Implementing a client/server network

We turn now to the basics of client/server networking at a scale suited to the small business. We will be using the Linux-based SME 7 server which can be downloaded from www.contribs.org. SME 7 is released under the General Public Licence and may be used without payment.

Hardware compatibility

Most current Linux distributions will run on most hardware, but if there is any doubt about support for any of your kit you can easily check on the Web. SME 7 is based on CentOS Linux and fully compatible with it. CentOS is, in turn, developed from 'a prominent North American Linux vendor', so the Red Hat Linux hardware compatibility list is worth consulting. There are also FAQs on various aspects of the system on the contribs.org website and a helpful user forum.

Settings

During the installation process you will need to provide IP addresses and a name for your server: have these to hand, along with any passwords or settings needed for Internet access.

Download the iso image

Like most Linux-based software, SME 7 is available as a download in iso format. Visit the site, follow the necessary links and download the version that you require. The version used in this chapter was made from the file smeserver-7.0.iso obtained though the contribs.org site. Before you can use it, *any* iso image has to be burnt to CD or DVD disk and this is not done by standard copying methods.

This example uses Nero burning software to create a bootable installation disk, though similar tools are available in other burning software.

1 Put a blank recordable CD disk in your CD writer drive.

2 Start the Nero software through the StartSmart menu item. This will present you with some options.

Figure 12.01

3 Click on the **Burn Image to Disk** option from the Copy and Backup menu. This will take you to a standard Windows file finding box.

4 Navigate to your iso image(s) and select the one that you want to burn.

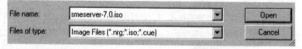

Figure 12.02

5 Click **Open** and follow the prompts until you are done.

6 Remove the new, bootable, CD from the drive and label it.

There are notes on using other CD burning software – Easy CD, CDR Win, WinOnCD and CD Burner XP Pro – on the contribs.org website.

Installing SME 7

SME 7 uses a text-based installer which is a bit fiddly to use until you are used to it, but it will run on almost any hardware and is very similar to the installers for other Linux-based products. With this in mind, we will do a text-based install, mainly using the defaults, then fine-tune it later using the web interface.

WARNING: the SME 7 installer will remove *all* partitions on both master and slave hard disks. If you have any data on any disk or partition, back it up or lose it.

Having set your CMOS/BIOS settings so you can boot from CD:

1 Put the installation CD in the drive and restart the PC. This will start a typical Linux boot sequence – a lot of white character output on a black screen – which will take you to a Welcome screen.

   You will now be given the opportunity to check the validity of the installation disk – a checksum calculation that ensures that the image was not corrupted in the download process. If this is your first use of this copy of the installer disk it is worth spending a couple of minutes running the media check.

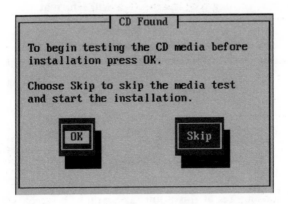

Figure 12.03

2 With the disk check complete (or skipped) the next step is to choose your installation language. Figure 12.04 is a good example of how the text-based installer works. You choose from the list (in this case languages) using the arrow keys,

then navigate between options by using [**Tab**] to go forwards and [**Alt**] + [**Tab**] to go backwards. Choose your language, tab forward to **OK**, then hit [**Enter**] to proceed.

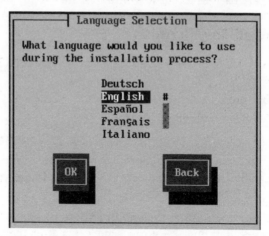

Figure 12.04

3 At the next prompt, select the keyboard layout for your country, then select **OK**. This will take you to a screen which gives you a warning that the installer will reformat all partitions.

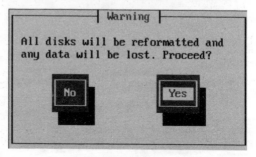

Figure 12.05

4 Choosing **Yes** at this point takes you to a screen where you can choose your time zone. Make your selection, tab to **OK** and hit [**Enter**] to start the main system installer. Depending on the speed of your system this may take between 10 and 20 minutes.

The install will proceed without further user intervention

until, on completion, it ejects the installation CD and asks you to reboot the PC.

5 Remove the installation CD and select **Reboot**.

Post-install configuration

This, too, is a text-based operation. Navigate between screens providing information as needed.

1 The first prompt is for an Administrator password. Choose something suitable, and then confirm it.

2 Set your domain name – in this example it is *newham.lan*. Choose **Next** to continue.

3 Choose your server name – here *Excalibur*. Choose **Next**.

4 Set the Local IP address for the server. This should be a static IP address – probably a class C network – and should be compatible with any addressing scheme that you already use. In this example, it is set to 192.168.2.250. Choose **Next**.

5 At the next screen you will see that the subnet mask has been entered for you. Choose **Next**.

6 You will be given a choice of operation mode. Change this to **Server-only** (we'll look at other modes later) and select **Next**.

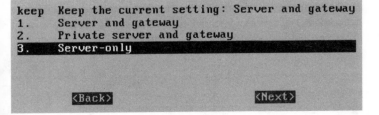

```
keep   Keep the current setting: Server and gateway
1.     Server and gateway
2.     Private server and gateway
3.     Server-only

        <Back>                        <Next>
```

Figure 12.06

7 You will be asked for the IP address of the Internet gateway. Here it is the address of a local router 192.168.2.1. Enter the address of your gateway and select **Next** to continue.

8 At the next screen you will be asked about running a DHCP server. Change this to **Off**. Select **Next** to continue.

```
keep   Keep the current setting: On
On     Provide DHCP service to local network
Off    Do not provide DHCP service to local network
```

Figure 12.07

9 Unless you have very good reason to do so, follow the suggestion that you leave the next screen blank. Click **Next**.

10 Finally, you will be asked: 'Do you wish to activate your changes?' Hit [**Enter**] to accept the default value of **Yes**. The system will now apply your settings. After a few minutes, the system will re-start, and you will be presented with a Linux login prompt in the form of your server name.

```
excalibur login: _
```

Figure 12.08

Don't panic. You will seldom need to work at a prompt. Most day-to-day management tasks can be done over your LAN using a web browser. We will return to command line work later.

Configuring and managing your SME server

Once you server software has been installed, you can carry out most management tasks from any Windows PC on your network, using a web browser such as Firefox or Internet Explorer. To do this, the Windows PC needs to be attached to the same network as the server and if necessary you can do this by using a crossover cable and a temporary static IP for the Windows PC.

With your PC connected to the network, you can test for connectivity by using the PING command with the IP address of the server as its argument. Figure 12.09 shows a satisfactory ping of the IP address of the server in the previous example.

```
C:\>PING 192.168.2.250

Pinging 192.168.2.250 with 32 bytes of data:

Reply from 192.168.2.250: bytes=32 time=1ms TTL=64
Reply from 192.168.2.250: bytes=32 time<1ms TTL=64
Reply from 192.168.2.250: bytes=32 time<1ms TTL=64
Reply from 192.168.2.250: bytes=32 time<1ms TTL=64

Ping statistics for 192.168.2.250:
    Packets: Sent = 4, Received = 4, Lost = 0 (0% loss),
Approximate round trip times in milli-seconds:
    Minimum = 0ms, Maximum = 1ms, Average = 0ms
```

Figure 12.09

How to access the management tools

With basic connectivity established you can now use your browser to access the 'webmin' interface of the server box:

1 Open a web browser window.

2 Type in the IP address of the server as shown in Figure 12.10, substituting the IP address of your server.

> https://192.168.2.250/server-manager

Figure 12.10

3 Skip any warning about security certificates. You will be prompted for a user name – this should be *admin* – and the password which you provided during installation. Click **OK** to go to the main server manager page. Choosing the menu entry to **Review configuration** will display a summary screen.

SME Server™
Server manager

admin@excalibur.newham.lan

Collaboration
Users
Groups
Quotas
Pseudonyms
Information bays

Administration
Backup or restore
View log files
Mail log file analysis
Reboot or shutdown

Security
Remote access
Local networks
Port forwarding
Proxy settings

Configuration
Software installer
Date and time
Workgroup
Directory
Printers
Hostnames and addresses
Domains
E-mail
Antivirus (ClamAV)
Review configuration

Miscellaneous
Support and licensing

Review configuration

Networking Parameters

Server Mode	serveronly
Local IP address / subnet mask	192.168.2.250/255.255.255.0
Gateway	192.168.2.1
Additional local networks	192.168.2.0/255.255.255.0
DHCP server	disabled

Server names

DNS server	192.168.2.250
Web server	www.newham.lan
Proxy server	proxy.newham.lan:3128
FTP server	ftp.newham.lan
SMTP, POP, and IMAP mail servers	mail.newham.lan

Domain information

Primary domain	newham.lan
Virtual domains	newham.lan
Primary web site	http://www.newham.lan
Server manager	https://excalibur/server-manager/
User password panel	https://excalibur/user-password/
Email Addresses	*useraccount*@newham.lan *firstname.lastname*@newham.lan *firstname_lastname*@newham.lan

SME Server 7.0

Figure 12.11

This might be a good time to spend a few minutes familiarizing yourself with the server–manager interface. In this chapter we will be using the entries for: users, remote access, and workgroup. We will look at printers in Chapter 13, *Printing*.

12.4 Setting up your workgroup server

The default installation that you carried out has already done most of the work for you. All you need to do is to access the server–manager page (Tip: why not make a Desktop shortcut to it?) and click on the **Workgroup** entry in the menu on the left. The default value for the workgroup field is 'mitel-networks'. Substitute your chosen workgroup name and click **Save**.

If you navigate to **My Network Places > View Workgroup Computers** on any XP box in the workgroup, you'll see the new server.

Figure 12.12

12.5 Adding user accounts

1 Access the server–manager page as 'admin'.

2 Select **Users** from the menu on the left.

3 Click **Add User Account**. This opens a form. Required fields are: **Account name** (all lower case), **First name** and **Last name**. All other fields are optional. Click **Add** and the system will confirm that the new account has been created.

Account name	anthony
First name	Anthony
Last name	Price

Figure 12.13

Note, from Figure 12.14, that the new account is locked and needs its password to be reset before it can be used.

Account	User name	VPN Client Access	Action			
admin	Local Administrator	No	Modify	Reset password		
anthony	Anthony Price	No	Modify	**Reset password**	Account is locked	Remove

Figure 12.14

4 Click on **Reset password** to open the Reset password dialog box.

Reset user password

You are about to change the password for the user account "anthony"
Enter the new password in the fields below

| New password | ******** |
| New password (verify) | ******** |

Figure 12.15

5 Click on the **Save** button and the account will be created. Note: by default SME 7 requires you to use strong passwords.

Strong passwords

A strong password must be at least 7 characters long, contain at least one upper case letter, one lower case, one number and one non-alphanumeric character. Fr1day-9, for example, fulfils these requirements. It is good practice to use strong passwords, but you can relax these requirements. Go to a console prompt, log in as 'root' and type the command:

    config setprop passwordstrength Users none

You must use the exact capitalization and syntax shown. It will disable password strength checking and is bad practice, but you may find it useful to do this while you are experimenting with setting up the system. To reverse it, issue the same command but substitute 'normal' or 'strong' for 'none'.

12.6 Working from a command line

SME boots to a Linux command line. From here, you can log in as one of two special users, 'root' or 'admin'. To do this, you need the Administrator password that you set at install time.

The root account

This is the superuser account on every Linux and Linux-based system. You may occasionally need to access this to make relatively low-level changes to the system. The strong passwords example, above, is fairly typical of the way that you might need to use the root account.

To access the root account:

1 Type 'root' at a system prompt and press [**Enter**].

2 Enter the Administrator password at the password prompt and press [**Enter**].

You now have unlimited rights over the whole system. Proceed with caution.

The admin account

This account is also used to make changes to the system at a lower level than the server-management pages that you access through your browser. Typically, this account is used to make major configuration changes that will require a reboot of the server. Setting up a DHCP server (below) is a typical task that you would undertake using the text-based admin account.

To access the admin account:

1 Type 'admin' at a system prompt and press [**Enter**].

2 Enter the Administrator password at the password prompt and press [**Enter**].

This will take you to a text-based server console similar in its functions to the SME 7 installer.

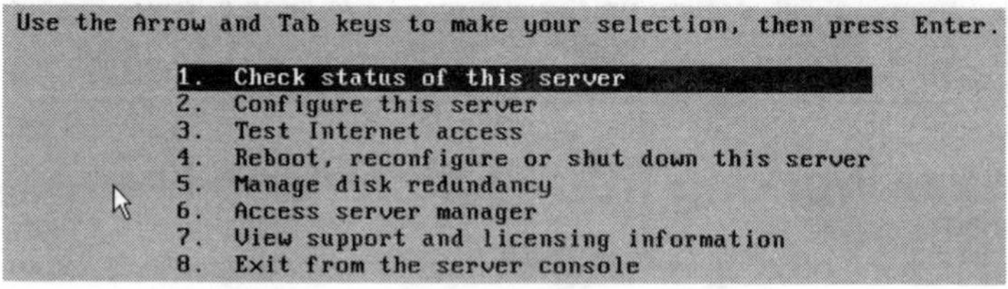

```
Use the Arrow and Tab keys to make your selection, then press Enter.

        1.  Check status of this server
        2.  Configure this server
        3.  Test Internet access
        4.  Reboot, reconfigure or shut down this server
        5.  Manage disk redundancy
        6.  Access server manager
        7.  View support and licensing information
        8.  Exit from the server console
```

Figure 12.16

12.7 How to access a command line from your desktop

It is common practice to run a production server without a monitor, or even without a keyboard and mouse. It is convenient, then, to be able to access your server's command line interface over your LAN. To make this possible, you will need to change some settings on your server, then download and install a secure shell client program.

The settings to change

By default, your server will not allow command line access over the LAN, so you need to enable this.

1 Use your browser to access the server–manager.

2 Click on the **Remote access** heading in the menu on the left of the page.

3 Change the **Secure Shell Settings** from their default values to those shown in Figure 12.17 and click **Save** (bottom right of the page) to save your choices.

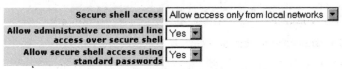

Figure 12.17

12.8 The secure shell client

The secure shell protocol exists to give secure command line access between machines. Whilst it is part of every Linux distribution, it is not native to Windows, so in order to use it you need to find and install a secure shell client program for Windows. There are many such programs available and a web search on the terms 'free secure shell client windows' will list several that are available. Alternatively, visit:

http://www.openssh.org/windows.html

Either way, finding a secure shell client program is the work of minutes. Moreover, these are small programs which will download quickly. The example which follows uses a free program PuTTY (the odd capitalization is deliberate, by the way) and with a file size of just 412KB it will download in seconds on a broadband connection. There is nothing to unpack, unzip or install. Just download it to a convenient location, click on the icon and use it.

1 Click on the PuTTY icon to launch the program.

2 Enter your server's IP address and press [Enter].

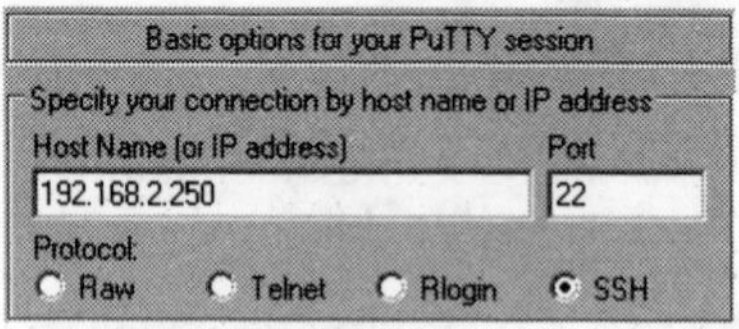

| Basic options for your PuTTY session |
| Specify your connection by host name or IP address |

Host Name (or IP address)   Port

192.168.2.250   22

Protocol:
○ Raw   ○ Telnet   ○ Rlogin   ● SSH

Figure 12.18

3 Skip any security warning and you will be presented with a standard Linux login prompt. From here you can log in using either of the privileged accounts – root or admin – just as if you were sitting at the server console.

12.9 How to configure a DHCP server

You should only have one DHCP server on your LAN. It may run on the main server box, or on its own dedicated hardware. Either way, its purpose is to allocate IP addresses to clients and it needs to be configured to suit your needs. Before you start, this may be a good time to turn back to Chapter 6, *Expanding your network*, which covers IP addressing schemes and DHCP.

In this example, we will access the server through the secure shell and set up the DCHP server to provide IP addresses in a range which we will define. What's needed is a DHCP pool of addresses which is reserved for dynamic allocations, with sufficient values left over – outside the scope of the pool – that can be used for devices, such as servers, that need static IP addresses.

1 Log in to your SME server using the admin account. This will take you to a text-based server console.

2 Select the option **Configure this server** and press [Enter].

3 Step through the various options – server name, address, etc., until you come to the option to configure the DHCP server. Use the arrow keys to set this to **On** and press [Enter].

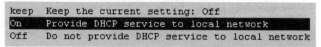
```
keep   Keep the current setting: Off
On     Provide DHCP service to local network
Off    Do not provide DHCP service to local network
```

Figure 12.19

4 At the next screens you are asked to specify the lower and upper boundaries of the DHCP range. Here, they have been set to give a DHCP pool of 192.168.2.100 to 192.168.2.200.

5 Step through the remainder of the server setup process and at the prompt **Do you wish to activate your changes?** Select **Yes**. Nothing will appear to happen. Your server will implement the changes, but in typically laconic Linux style it won't actually confirm this. You can, however, check that it has been done, by stepping through the setup process again, or running the IPCONFIG command on one of your client PCs.

201

client/server networks

12

```
Connection-specific DNS Suffix  . : newham.lan
IP Address. . . . . . . . . . . : 192.168.2.200
Subnet Mask . . . . . . . . . . : 255.255.255.0
Default Gateway . . . . . . . . : 192.168.2.1
```

Figure 12.20

Figure 12.20 shows the output of the IPCONFIG command. Note that the client PC's IP address is at the top of the DHCP range which we defined earlier. You now have a working server.

12.10 Setting up a gateway

The purpose of the gateway is to route traffic from the LAN to external networks such as the Internet. You can run a gateway on the same physical hardware (as in the next example) but there are strong security arguments in favour of using either a dedicated hardware router or a separate PC for this purpose. Do you *really* want your main file store attached directly to the Net?

Hardware

To function as a router/gateway your server needs to have two LAN cards: an external interface which is public (i.e. connects to the Internet) and an internal interface which is private and connects to your LAN. If you don't have two network cards, the first job is to fit a second card.

1 Power down the server and fit the card, probably in a PCI slot.

2 Reboot. Ignore any prompts to configure the new hardware. We will do that from a console prompt.

Configuring your gateway

1   Connect to your server console either directly or through a secure shell and log in as 'admin'.

2   Choose **Configure this server** and step through the various choices until you reach the screen to **Select operation mode**.

3   Select the **Private server and gateway** option.

4   At the next screen, confirm the default **Server and gateway – dedicated** option.

5   Select the external Ethernet card (the one you fitted earlier).

6   Select Static IP for this card.

7   Enter the IP address for this card – in this instance it is 192.168.3.5 – because this is compatible with an existing router on a different private network which connects to the Internet. Your settings will be different and will depend on how you connect to the Internet. Consult your documentation and ISP details to determine your settings.

8   Accept the default value for the subnet mask.

9   Enter the IP address of the gateway address of your Internet connection. In this instance it is 192.168.3.1 – the address of a local router. Again, check your documentation to find the correct address for your system.

10 Step through the remainder of the options, accepting the existing values for DHCP etc., then at the final screen, select the **Reboot** option.

Testing

Once your server has rebooted, run the IPCONFIG command from a prompt to check your new settings. Figure 12.21 shows the output for the example above.

```
Ethernet adapter Local Area Connection:

        Connection-specific DNS Suffix  . : newham.lan
        IP Address. . . . . . . . . . . . : 192.168.2.200
        Subnet Mask . . . . . . . . . . . : 255.255.255.0
        Default Gateway . . . . . . . . . : 192.168.2.250
```

Figure 12.21

As you can see from the figure, your client PC has an IP address assigned by the DHCP server and the gateway is set to the (static) IP address that you allocated to the *local* interface. When you request a web page, the request is passed to this local address and the gateway passes it in turn to the *external* interface. This means that the LAN is never directly attached to the Internet because your gateway PC translates requests from the internal interface to the format of the external interface – a process known as Network Address Translation (NAT). As a further test, use PING to test an Internet address or point the browser at a website.

12.11 Setting up a domain controller

Note: at the time of writing there are connectivity problems between Vista and the SME server software. These will doubtless be resolved, but if you are planning to deploy Vista clients, you will need to check on the status of this issue. The FAQs and help forums at contribs.org would be a good starting point for this.

On the server

1   Use your browser to access the server–manager page on your SME server.

2   Navigate to the **Workgroup** page and look at your settings. Figure 12.22 shows these for the server EXCALIBUR. On the server end of the connection, to make EXCALIBUR function as a domain controller change the entry in the **Workgroup and Domain Controller** field from **No** to **Yes** and click **Save**, at the bottom of the page.

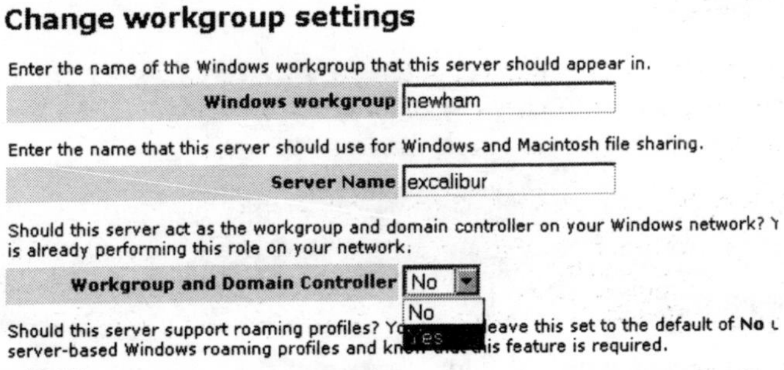

Change workgroup settings

Enter the name of the Windows workgroup that this server should appear in.

| Windows workgroup | newham |

Enter the name that this server should use for Windows and Macintosh file sharing.

| Server Name | excalibur |

Should this server act as the workgroup and domain controller on your Windows network? Y is already performing this role on your network.

Workgroup and Domain Controller	No
	No
	Yes

Should this server support roaming profiles? Yo   leave this set to the default of No u server-based Windows roaming profiles and kno   is feature is required.

Figure 12.22

On the client – editing the registry

To make connectivity possible between an XP PC and an SME server that is operating as a domain controller, you have to tweak one registry setting.

1   Start the Windows registry editor – type **regedit** at a prompt or in a 'run' box.

2   Navigate to: **HKEY_LOCAL_MACHINE\SYSTEM\ Current ControlSet\Services\Netlogon\parameters.**

Figure 12.23

3   The default value for **requiresignorseal** is 1. Double-click on this entry and change the value to 0 (zero).

4   Exit from the registry editor – there is no need to 'save' the change because registry updates are instantaneous.

On the client – joining the domain

1   Navigate to **My Computer > Properties > Computer Name** and click **Change.** This opens a dialog box where you can change the PC's name or its workgroup/domain membership. (Tip: don't try to change both at in a single operation – it will go wrong.)

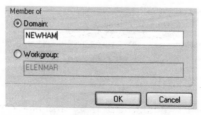

Figure 12.24

2   Enter the name of your domain in the appropriate box and

click **OK**. You will then be prompted for the name of an account with permission to join the domain.

3 Enter the user name admin and the password for that account on the SME server. Click **OK**. The system will pause for around half a minute (while it connects with the domain controller – your SME 7 box) before displaying a welcome notice. Click **OK** to join the domain.

Figure 12.25

4 The PC must be rebooted to complete the change. Step through the next couple of prompts, clicking **OK** until you are prompted to reboot the system. At the final prompt: 'Do you want to restart your computer now?' click **Yes** to reboot.

On the client – configuring user details

At the Windows logon prompt you will be give the choice to log on to the local machine or the domain.

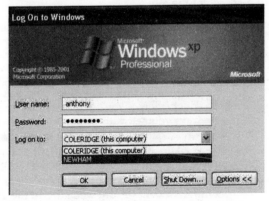

Figure 12.26

1 Log on to the domain, with name and password for a user – in this case 'anthony'. After verifying user name and password the system will let you in.

2 Click on **My Computer**. You will see that the system has automatically mapped the Z: drive to the user's account. This will happen for every user who has an account on the server.

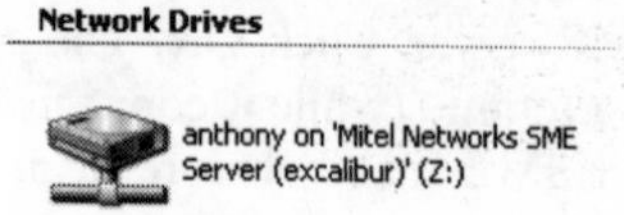

Network Drives

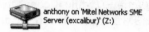

anthony on 'Mitel Networks SME
Server (excalibur)' (Z:)

Figure 12.27

3 Navigate to **My Documents > Properties > Target** folder and use **Move** to relocate it to the Z: drive, much as you did when setting up a shared file store in Chapter 2.

You will need to do this once for each user on the system, but not on each machine. One of the advantages of a domain is that a user can log into their account from anywhere on the network.

Summary

In this chapter we have considered the advantages and requirements for implementing a client/server network. We have looked in general terms at some of the services likely to be of interest to a small business and outlined the characteristics of some common network operating systems that can be used for the job.

We have scratched the surface of the possibilities of a client/server LAN using SME Server. We have looked at obtaining it, installing it and configuring it for various purposes.

However, if you really want to get to grips with it you will need to explore some of its other capabilities and assess their usefulness to your business. You could profitably spend some time familiarizing yourself with the options available through the server–manager. Look at the backup options, then re-read the Backup options section of Chapter 7. Repeat the exercise, assessing the possibilities of RAID – hint: SME supports software RAID free and 'out of the box'. And don't forget the www.contribs.org website and the user forums. Whatever the problem or the query, chances are that someone else has already experienced it and the answer will be available on the net.

13 printing

In this chapter you will learn:

- how to connect to a 'network-ready' printer

- how to set up a print server/access box

- how to use SME as a print server

13.1 Network printing

The simplest way of setting up network printing is to attach a printer to a local port – usually parallel or USB – on a Windows PC, then to share it over the network. (See section 2.4, *Sharing a printer*.) This has the advantage of being easy to set up and maintain and is usually sufficient to meet the needs of a small workgroup. It does, however, impose an overhead on the PC which is used to control the printer and if the volume of print jobs is large, or you want more control over print jobs and access, then you should consider some alternatives.

Using a network-ready printer

Some printers – particularly laser printers intended for commercial use – have a network interface built into them. A printer of this type will have an RJ45 port which allows direct connection to the network. Like any network device, a printer has a MAC address built into it and you need to assign an IP address to it in order to make it accessible on your network. The first thing you will need will be your printer manual. If you don't have one, visit the manufacturer's website and download a manual or setup guide, for your make and model.

Printers vary considerably between both makes and models, so this example, which applies to a Hewlett-Packard LaserJet, should be treated as an outline which may need to be adapted for your particular circumstances.

1 Disconnect the printer from the network, power down, then restart it.

2 Use the menu button to display – or print out – the current IP settings. You can probably find out how to do this by experimentation or you could, of course, read the manual.

3 Now that you know the printer's default IP address, connect a PC (or your laptop) to it with a crossover cable.

4 Assign a static IP address to the PC so that it has one which is compatible with that of the printer.

5 Type the IP address of the printer into the Address bar of your browser to access the printer's setup page.

6 Assign a static IP address and any other configuration details for the printer, making sure that these are compatible with your network. Save these settings.

7 Disconnect your temporary connection and reconnect your printer to your network.

8 Use the PING command with your new printer's IP address to test that it is visible on your network. If the IP address was 192.168.2.25, for example, you should enter this at a command line prompt:

    PING 192.2.25 [Enter]

The next step is to install the new printer on your PC clients – see *Installing the network printer on the client*, below.

13.2 Using a print server box

These are usually described as *print servers*, though most of them may be better described as access boxes as they do not store or manage print jobs. Basically, they provide an RJ45 to connect to the LAN, a power connection and a port to connect to a printer. Figure 13.01 shows an example of this type of device.

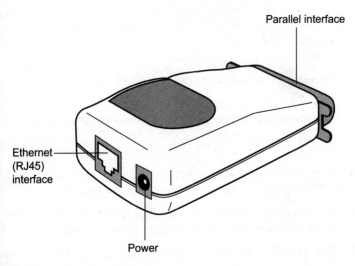

Parallel interface

Ethernet (RJ45) interface

Power

Figure 13.01 A print server box.

Like any Ethernet device, each server box has a unique MAC address which needs to have an IP address allocated to it. Setup methods vary between products, so the key is to obtain documentation from the manufacturer and follow the instructions. Major vendors have detailed help available on their websites.

Using SME server as a print server

This is very similar to setting up a network shared printer on a Windows PC. In this example we will attach an Epson ink jet to the parallel port on the server, though the system supports all printer types, and other local port types such as USB.

1 Attach your printer to a port on the SME server box.

2 Connect to the server through the server–manager interface.

3 Click on the **Printers** entry on the main menu.

4 Click **Add Printer** to open the **Add Printer** dialog box.

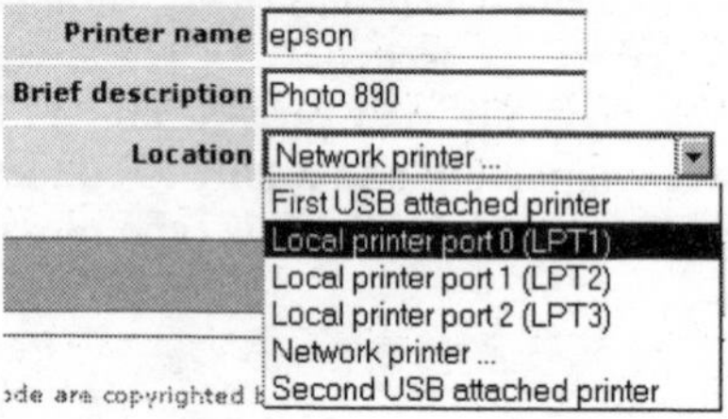

Figure 13.02

5 Enter a name for the printer, a brief description, and select the port to which it is attached from the drop-down list.

6 Click **Add.** The system will take half a minute or so to add the printer. When it is done it will confirm the installation.

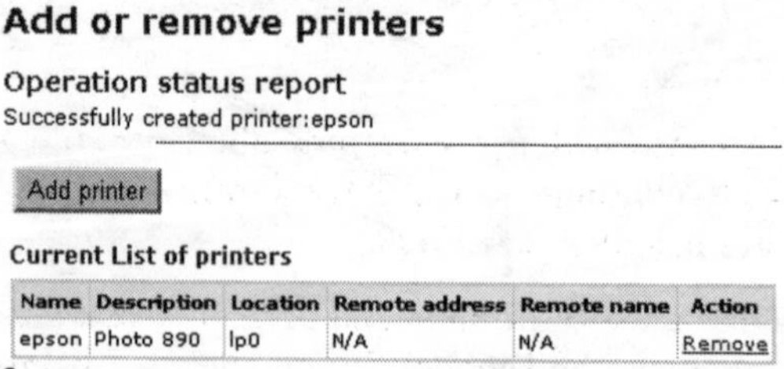

Figure 13.03

You now need to install the printer on your client PCs.

13.3 Installing a network printer on a client

This is done using the Add Printer Wizard and the steps vary according to the type of printer. The process isn't helped much by Microsoft's rather confusing terminology, so we need to clarify this before proceeding. In terms of the Add Printer Wizard:

- A *network printer* is one attached to a port on a host on the network. For that host, of course, the printer is local.

- A *printer with an IP address* – which most of us would call a network printer – is treated as a special type of local printer.

Installing a network printer

1 Start the Add Printer Wizard.

2 Choose **Network Printer**, and click on **Next** to browse.

3 After a few seconds, the system will show a list of available printers. In this case we are interested in the Epson Photo 890 on the server Excalibur – the one we installed earlier.

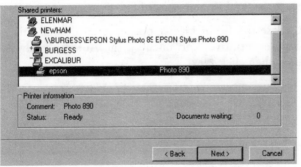

Figure 13.04

4 Click **Next**. You will see a warning about installing drivers. Click **Yes** to continue. You will see another warning, that no drivers are installed. Click **OK**.

5 You will see a list of printers and drivers. Scroll down it and select your make and model. If you see your printer listed, click **OK** to install the drivers, otherwise use the **Have Disk** option and install drivers from the manufacturer's disk.

Figure 13.05

On exit, the Wizard will show you the new printer, and you will
have the opportunity to set it as the default and to print a test page.

13.4 Installing a printer that has its own IP address

The XP printer wizard

1   Start the Add Printer Wizard.

2   Choose the *Local Printer* option, even though this may be
    counter-intuitive, and uncheck the **Automatically detect...**
    box, then click **Next**.

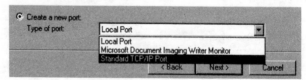

Figure 13.06

3   Choose **Create a new port**. Choose **Standard TCP/IP port**
    and click **Next**. This starts the TCP/IP Printer Port Wizard.

4   Check that your target printer (or access box) has a valid IP
    address for your network and that it is powered up and con-
    nected. Click **Next**.

5   Enter the IP address of the printer or device. The system will
    use this as the basis of the port name. Other choices are pos-

sible, but if you stick with the IP address, the system is, in effect, self-documented. Click **Next**.

Enter the Printer Name or IP address, and a port name for the desired device.

Printer Name or IP Address: 192.168.2.25

Port Name: IP_192.168.2.25

Figure 13.07

6   If you entered a valid IP address and the printer is connected and on, all you have to do now is to step though the remaining options – installing drivers, etc. – as you would for a local printer. If it is not recognized, check for physical connectivity, then check settings such as the IP address and start again.

The Vista printer wizard

The Vista version of the wizard is similar in operation to its XP counterpart, though it is rather better than XP at detecting and configuring printers – especially local printers connected to a USB port. To use the wizard, navigate to **Control Panel > Hardware and Sound > Printers**, then click **Add a printer**.

> Control Panel > Hardware and Sound > Printers

Organize ▾   Views ▾   Add a printer

Figure 13.08

The dialog box to set up a TCP/IP port for printing is similar to XP, though, once again, Vista tends to be better at auto detecting hardware and organizing drivers.

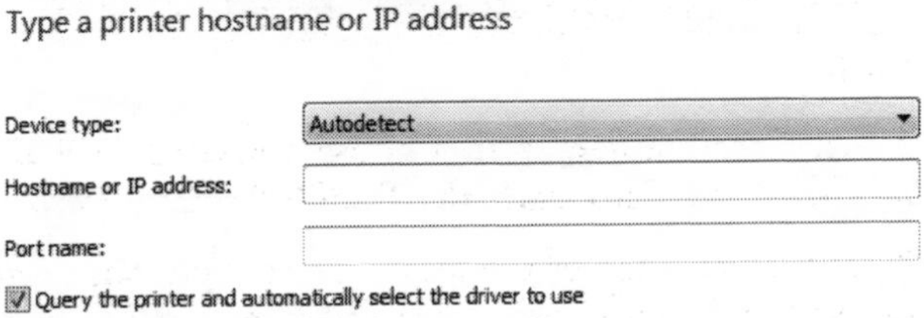

Type a printer hostname or IP address

Device type: Autodetect

Hostname or IP address:

Port name:

☑ Query the printer and automatically select the driver to use

Figure 13.09

If Vista doesn't find your printer, you can enter the IP address manually and proceed as outlined in the XP example above.

Summary

This chapter has examined the basics of printing over a small network. We have considered the basic Windows share method of printing, printing with SME server, and attaching to print devices which have their own IP addresses. With the information in this chapter you should have little problem in implementing and maintaining network printing services on your LAN.

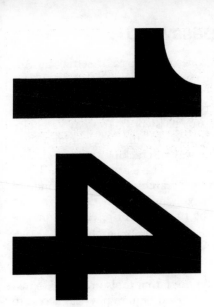

In this chapter you will learn:

- how to crack an XP/Vista password

- how to implement physical security measures

- how to implement administrative security policies

14.1 Cracking a password

When you install Windows, one of the tasks is setting an Administrator password for the system. When creating an answer file to use for an unattended install you probably chose the option to encrypt it as a security precaution. What happens if you lose or forget the Administrator password? You have a choice between either reinstalling Windows – time-consuming to say the least – or of finding some way of cracking the password in order to gain access to the system. There are lawful and legitimate tools for doing this. A web search on the term 'Windows password recovery' will show you any number of paid-for and free tools which will allow you to recover or reset the Administrator password on any NT-based Windows system: XP, Vista, Server 2003 as well as older Windows releases such as Windows 2000 and its server versions.

Most of the password recovery/resetting tools are Linux-based bootable disks – floppy or CD – and require physical access to the target PC.

The example which follows uses a free utility written by Petter Nordahl-Hagen. It is available in both floppy and CD-ROM formats and needs to be downloaded and copied to the appropriate disk type. As many systems these days don't even have a floppy drive, we will look at the CD version.

Creating the bootable CD

1 Download the CD version of the program. It is compressed in .zip format, so the first job is to unzip it. This will leave you with an .iso file that needs to be burnt to CD.

2 Use a CD burning program to make a bootable CD. Chapter 12 showed you how to do this using Nero burning software.

3 Check that the burn process has been successful by navigating to the CD drive on your PC to check that you have the correct files – not just a copy of the .iso. You should see something like Figure 14.01.

Name
Files Currently on the CD
BOOT.CAT
BOOT.MSG
INITRD.GZ
ISOLINUX.BIN
ISOLINUX.CFG
VMLINUZ

Figure 14.01

If you can only see a single .iso file, re-read the relevant part of Chapter 12 and try again.

Using the CD

Bearing in mind that this is free software that comes entirely without warranty and that it does not work on encrypted file systems, this is how you reset your password.

1 Boot to the CD – you may have to change the boot order in CMOS setup to do this – and read the legal disclaimer.

2 Follow the on-screen prompts, accepting default values until you reach the prompt to reset the Windows Administrator password. (You can get to this stage of the process simply by pressing [Enter] to accept default values.)

Figure 14.02

3 When you are prompted for a new Administrator password, follow the on-screen suggestion and set it to * (an asterisk) which will set the password to [Enter] when you reboot to Windows.

4 At the next prompt, you will be asked if you 'Really wish to change it'. You will need to change the default answer of 'no' to 'yes' by entering 'Y' at the prompt and pressing [Enter].

5 At the next prompt, enter an exclamation mark and press [Enter].

6 At the next prompt, enter 'q' to quit.

7 You will now see a final prompt: 'About to write file(s) back. Do it?' The default value here is 'n'. Change this to 'y', and then press [Enter]. The system will report success and offer you the chance to repeat the process. The default here is 'n' so press [Enter] to accept it.

8 Remove the bootable CD from the drive and press [Ctrl] + [Alt] + [Del] to restart the Windows system.

9 On reboot, Windows will run the CHKDSK utility – which you can skip, if you wish – and boot normally.

10 At the Windows logon prompt enter the user name 'Administrator' and leave the password field blank. Press [**Enter**] and you're in. You have full administrator rights over the local PC and can reset other users' passwords, make system changes and so on.

As described, our password cracker is a useful tool. It can save you from a reinstall of Windows in the event of a lost Administrator password. However, the fact that it works equally well with a Windows-based server, presents us with a security problem. What you can do legitimately can also be done by someone else for malicious reasons, hence the need for physical security.

14.2 Physical security

Whatever physical security measures you decide on, it is as well to bear in mind that small business is not really at significant risk from international crime syndicates, but rather from opportunistic thieves, most of whom are none too bright to begin with. Simple common sense precautions are probably sufficient to deter most would-be thieves and should be as visible as possible.

The server room

We have already seen some advantages of using a single PC as a workgroup or domain-based file server: ease of administration, centralized backups, etc. We may now add physical security to the list. With all data held on one PC, you can concentrate your physical security efforts on this key piece of hardware. At the least, the server should be in a locked room with the minimum of access allowed to non-IT staff. Large network installations often employ swipe-card technology to restrict access to a particular group of employees and to monitor staff access, which may be supplemented by CCTV cameras and recordings. This may be impractical for a small business, though a camera prominently fixed over a door can be a considerable deterrent.

The minimum security for a server room is, of course, a lockable door. If you choose a keypad lock, make sure that the number is known only to those who need to know and that it is changed from time to time (say once a month, perhaps). The easiest locking system is, perhaps, a good quality mortice lock with one key kept by the System Administrator and the other in a safe in another office or off-site altogether.

Security marking components

Many of the thefts of computer equipment are not commercial or industrial espionage so much as the hi-tech equivalent of car theft. PCs and their components are stolen, 'refurbished' and sold on in the second-hand market. Your business information – priceless to you – is lost, even though the thief gains only a few hundred pounds for the second-hand hardware. An obvious disincentive to this type of theft is clear security marking of all your equipment. This may take the form of asset tags fixed to system boxes, postcode 'tattooing' of cases and/or ultra-violet pen markers which can be used on internal components. If your hard disk, for example, has your post code written on it using even a basic security pen, it is not nearly so saleable as its unmarked equivalent. A label to this effect, prominently displayed on the machine, may provide an effective disincentive to theft.

14.3 Administrative security

Many of the security threats that you face on your network come from outside your LAN. Every time you open a port on your firewall or offer a service like running your own mail or web server you increase your vulnerability. That is not to say that you shouldn't use e-mail or have a website, just that you should proceed with care and, where possible, have such services hosted externally. As for remote access for your users – do they really need it? Unless it is carefully configured, managed and monitored your system will be vulnerable to outside attack.

Viruses and malware

Viruses and other malware have been considered in Chapter 9 *Internet and e-mail*, and these are probably the most important external threats. Keep your scanners and other software up to date. You also have an important job to do in raising awareness in your users. You may, for example, have a policy about bringing disks in from outside, personal e-mail, etc., but you should also have a 'no-fault' virus reporting policy. If users think that they will be reprimanded for reporting a problem then they will be less likely to do so and a PC virus – like a biological one – needs early intervention if problems are to be minimized.

Password policies

Complex passwords are difficult to guess or to crack using brute force methods. Guidelines for passwords should consider:

◆ Length – less than (say) 7 characters are too easy to crack

◆ Dictionary words are susceptible to attack

◆ Personal names. If you use your middle name, your spouse's name or the name of your dog, then it's not too difficult for someone else to guess.

◆ Avoid the obvious – *Password* or *drowssap* for instance have both been used a million times at least.

A good password, then, is one that is easy for the user to remember, but difficult for anyone else to guess or crack, and the 'easy to remember' part is important. On Windows servers for example, you can force complexity rules on your users and make them change their password from time to time. However, if you overdo it – insist on a 36-character password that must include letters, numbers and punctuation marks, for example – then users will write them down and keep them on their desks. Not much security there.

By default SME enforces strong passwords (see page 197). You can override this requirement if you wish, but it may be better to persuade your users that they are worthwhile. Beware of the user who feels that his (or her) data is 'not important' – this is usually just false humility – 'who would be interested in lil 'ol me?' The fact is that one weak (or known) password is a security threat to the whole network.

Encourage your users to change their passwords from time to time. On Windows systems, hold down [Ctrl] + [Alt] + [Del] and select **Change Password** to access the password changing dialog box. On SME systems, log in, and then point the browser to <IP address of your server>/user-password. This can be used by anyone to change their own password. An administrator can also log in to the server–manager and reset anyone's for them.

Use more than one server box

From a security point of view, running your gateway and or firewall services on the same server box as your shared file store is not best practice. You can deploy separate servers for functions such as gateway, firewall and DHCP and keep your file server entirely inside your LAN, i.e. without a *direct* connection to the Internet.

Even if you are using a paid-for server system for your main file server/domain controller, you can still provide gateway/firewall/DHCP through one or more Linux-based systems deployed for these purposes. In addition to SME, there are a couple of other Linux-based free products for gateway/firewall/DHCP such as Smoothwall and IPCOP – a web search on either of these terms will take you to their respective sites.

Summary

For the small business, in particular, you need to ask; 'How much is enough?' You can't do everything, and neither should you. You don't need the same levels of security as a national government or an international bank – the threat level is simply not the same. Implement some sensible practices and policies – physical security, sensible password policies and up-to-date anti-virus measures. Above all, involve your users. Security is everyone's concern.

15

documentation and training

In this chapter you will learn:

- about the need for documentation

- about user training

- about training for yourself

15.1 The need for documentation

Documentation should start at the very earliest stages of setting up your network. You need to record the physical layout of your network, the cable runs, the location of the PCs, servers, etc. You also need to have a record of addressing schemes and naming conventions. If, for example, you know that the DCHP range is set up as (say) 192.168.2.100 to 192.168.2.200 and that server machines are in the range below this and end in a zero, running IPCONFIG on a machine will tell you both its address and its role in the network.

All changes to the network should also be documented. If you add a PC or a user account, details need to be noted for future reference. Repairs, additions and the outcomes of troubleshooting exercises also need to be recorded. This information needs to be kept in permanent form with at least one copy stored off site. It may also be advisable to keep an ink on paper print of the information in a file somewhere. In the event of a catastrophic failure the network will have to be rebuilt, its functionality and its data restored. That's quite an undertaking to carry out from memory, even if you built the whole system yourself. It is an order of magnitude more difficult if someone else has the task of rebuilding it, or you face the task of rebuilding someone else's system.

The general rule, then, is a simple one: plan what you are going to do, do it, and document it. The day will come when you'll be glad you did.

15.2 Training for your users

Another use for documentation is that it can provide the basis for staff training. Whilst there are general training courses available on just about every aspect of computing and ICT, the specifics of your system are unique to you and your documentation captures those unique features.

Training for a new system

When you are planning and implementing your network it can be useful to involve your users as much as possible in the planning process. When you first implement your network, set up a couple of machines to run the new system and have brief training sessions – two or three staff at a time – in the basics of how to log on, use and exit from the new system. Users often dislike the new, simply *because* it is new. A couple of hours of unpressured introduction to the system away from the pressures of real work can be beneficial. A further benefit is the opportunity for you to fine-tune the system to meet the users' needs – if everyone finds it difficult to carry out a particular task then you can change it. Not only will you have responded to your users' perceived needs, but you will have been seen to do so. Goodwill from the users is an intangible but very real benefit when running a network.

New users on an existing system

Most companies have some form of induction programme for new members of staff and as part of this they should be introduced to the working of the network. They will need a user name and a password. They will need to be shown how to log on and off, how to access their files, connect to the Internet, and where and how to print. It is probably a good idea to prepare some sort of 'handout' of these details. Not only will this be useful for the new member of staff (who has quite enough to cope with on day one of a new job) but it will also sharpen your appreciation of what is needed – explaining something to someone else is often a useful exercise in clarifying your own thinking.

Reporting procedures

Any networked workplace needs procedures to report faults. On a large corporate network this can be quite a formal procedure, possibly even filling in a form or sending an e-mail to a particular address which organizes fault reports and their resolutions through a ticketing system. In a smaller organization, this is probably excessive. However, there still need to be some simple guidelines for reporting faults. Every user should know:

* The person responsible for taking fault reports – name, e-mail address or other contact details.

* To note and report any error messages that accompany the fault or failure.

- To check basics like whether or not the machine is turned on at the mains.

- To reboot their workstation before making a support call.

225

documentation and training

15

Obviously you can expand or alter this list to suit your own needs, your system and your users. The object of the exercise is to have a clear, consistent user-friendly reporting procedure that will enable you to deal with problems quickly and effectively – and, of course, to document the problems and their solutions. You can, over time, accumulate a knowledge base of faults and solutions, some of which may even feed into long-term improvements to the system as a whole.

15.3 Training for you

Nothing in computing – and particularly in networking – stays the same for long. Today's leading edge/bleeding edge may well turn out to be tomorrow's mainstream technology, so you need to keep up.

Where there are relevant training courses available at, for example, a local college, you should ask for day release from work to attend them. The Computer Technology Industry Association (CompTIA) Network+ examination certifies the skills of a network technician with 9 months on-the-job experience. It is an American qualification, but it is recognized worldwide. In the United Kingdom, Network+ is administered by the OCR exam board and may attract government funding, if taken through a college. You may also like to consider other, less formal courses. Colleges may provide introductory network courses which may or may not be linked to a formal qualification.

There are also, vendor-specific qualifications: Novell, Microsoft and Red Hat all have certification programmes in the specifics of their products.

For the free Open Source systems there are support sites and help forums and, if you want to expand your knowledge of Linux, there are many books, specialist magazines and websites. There is also, as you might expect, a *Teach Yourself* book on Linux. This is particularly good on command-line work – useful for some tasks on a Linux-based server.

Summary

This chapter has considered the related topics of documentation and user training during the setup phase of a new network. It has also considered the training needs of new users on an established network, with particular emphasis on procedures for reporting network faults. Finally, we have considered your training needs. Managing even a small network is a considerable responsibility, especially when things go wrong. Accurate documentation and adequate training may be unglamorous, but so is a fire extinguisher – until you have a fire.

16

troubleshooting

In this chapter you will learn:

- the principles of troubleshooting
- the questions to ask
- the tools to use

16.1 Principles

Both networks and the PCs that make them up will fail from time to time. There are a finite number of things that can go wrong and you converge on a solution by asking questions, listing possibilities, and testing them one by one.

Start with the obvious

Many faults with PCs – networked or otherwise – arise from really simple things: loose connectors, lack of power, incorrect passwords, so the first step in troubleshooting is to check the obvious. Does the faulty device – PC, printer, router, whatever – have power and a connection to the network?

1 Check for mains power.

2 Reseat any cables that may be loose.

3 Reboot.

All devices on your network have volatile RAM memory and this can become corrupted or misallocated in the course of day-to-day operations. The cure for this is simply to reboot the device. This will restore the contents of RAM and can fix many problems. If it doesn't fix the problem, you will have eliminated one of the possibilities, and that is *the* key to successful fault diagnosis – patient, systematic investigation of the possibilities and eliminating them one by one until a solution is found.

Ask the user

Most investigations will start with a user report of a problem. If you are advising over the phone, you will need to note the user's name and location and the nature of the problem. Unless there is a complete network failure, ask the user to reboot the device and see if that fixes the problem. If it does, you have both been spared a call out. If it doesn't, you have eliminated one possibility.

If you are providing deskside support, then reboot the device, and if this doesn't fix the problem, ask:

♦ What has changed?

♦ When did the problem start?

♦ Does anyone else use the device?

These questions may provide some pointers to the underlying causes of the problem.

What has changed?

Systems that are working tend to go on working. Where a system has been changed – new software or a hardware upgrade or replacement – and it subsequently fails, then a strong candidate for the cause has to be the change which preceded the failure. Fortunately, this is easy to diagnose – undo the recent change and see if it fixes the problem. In practice, this may mean removing a suspect hardware component, uninstalling software or even using the System Restore feature of Windows to roll back to a previously known good state.

When did the problem start?

If the system went from working to not working at a definite time, but there have been no known changes, you are probably looking at a hardware failure. If, on the other hand, the system has been deteriorating over time, then it is more likely to be an operating system fault or a virus infection. Note that we are considering possibilities and probabilities when troubleshooting – drawing firm conclusions on the basis of too little evidence is probably the biggest trap that you face: 'Certainty is the enemy of enquiry'.

Does anyone else use the device?

If anyone else uses the device – PC, printer, whatever – then your list of questions to the user who reported the fault is less than complete. The 'anyone else' question is really a part of the 'Don't forget the obvious' guideline.

Reproduce the problem

The most important request to the user is 'Show me'. If you haven't already done so, reboot the machine and ask the user to demonstrate the problem. Check that they are logging in to the system with a correct user name and password and note any error message that may be displayed at the point of failure.

Isolate the problem

The commonest reported problem from users is the inability to log in to the network. A useful step in determining whether this is a node problem, a network problem, or a user account problem, is twofold.

1 Log in to the network using your own credentials. If you can log in, but the user can't, then the hardware is functioning properly. If possible, you should log in as a non-privileged user rather than using your administrative or 'root' privileged account.

2 Ask the user to log in from another node on the network. If he or she can log in from a different point on the network, then the problem is with the PC. If not, then it is probably a password problem. Try resetting the user's password and ask them to try again.

16.2 The troubleshooting tools

Link lights

All network devices have LEDs which indicate their status. The number, position and meaning of the LEDs will vary from device to device, but one of them will be a Link Light – this should be lit for a device that is working. Other lights will flicker to indicate the movement of data packets across the interface. Even if you don't know the exact meaning of each light without looking in the manual, lack of lights altogether suggests power failure or hardware failure. In the case of a PC's network card, the obvious next step is to change the NIC.

Spare network card

These are cheap enough to buy, so you should carry a few spares – preferably a make and model that will plug and play out of the box. If there are no lights on the existing card, power down and replace with a new one. Power up, configure as necessary for your network, and then try again. If this works, fine. If not, you may well have a cable problem.

Spare cable

The patch cables which attach the workstation PCs to the wall jacks are a common point of failure. Replacing a suspect patch cable with a known good replacement is the work of a few seconds. Another useful tool is a spare crossover cable. Detach the workstation from the network and connect to a spare PC or a laptop with a crossover cable. If, with a new NIC and a known good patch cable you can't connect to the network, but you *can* connect over a crossover cable, then you are probably looking at a problem with your main premises cabling.

PING

The software tool PING is available on all operating systems – including Windows – for diagnosing TCP/IP networks. You can ping a remote system by name or by IP address. If you can't ping a device on your network, then you have a basic connectivity problem – check cable, card and configuration, in that order.

If you successfully ping by name, the command will show the numeric IP address of the remote machine. If you ping across the Internet, and you find that you can ping a site by its IP address but not its name, then you probably have an incorrect setting for the Domain Name Service (DNS) so check your settings against those given to you by your ISP.

NET VIEW

The NET command has many functions – type NET /? at a command prompt for help on its uses – but the one that interests us here is the VIEW option. Unlike PING – which is part of TCP/IP and therefore cross-platform – NET VIEW is a Windows command and will list Windows machines and compatible servers such as SME 7 in your current Windows Workgroup, but not other devices such as hardware routers or network printers. Figure 15.01 shows the output of NET VIEW on a small network.

```
\\ASIMOU
\\BURGESS              Development PC - main office
\\COLERIDGE
\\VICTORIA             elenmar file server
The command completed successfully.
```

Figure 15.01

Note the **Remark** field in the output. This shows the contents of the **Description** field that is part of the target PC's properties. (Right-click on **My Computer**, select **Properties** from the context menu and select the **Computer Name** tab.)

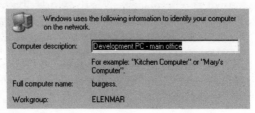

Figure 15.02

Clearly, the information in this field can be useful when troubleshooting.

IPCONFIG

The IPCONFIG command can be used at a system prompt to show the current configuration of the system. Every node on your network needs to be on the 'same' network – i.e. have an IP address and settings that are compatible with everything else. Suppose, for example, you have checked cable and card and established that you have connectivity at the hardware level, then a possible cause may be wrong settings. Use IPCONFIG to check them. On a network which uses DHCP to allocate IP addresses you can use this command to obtain a new IP address like this:

1 IPCONFIG /RELEASE – clears the current settings.

2 IPCONFIG /RENEW – obtains new settings from the DHCP server.

3 IPCONFIG – to view the new settings.

If the output of this command resembles that of Figure 15.03 then you have a problem connecting with your DHCP server.

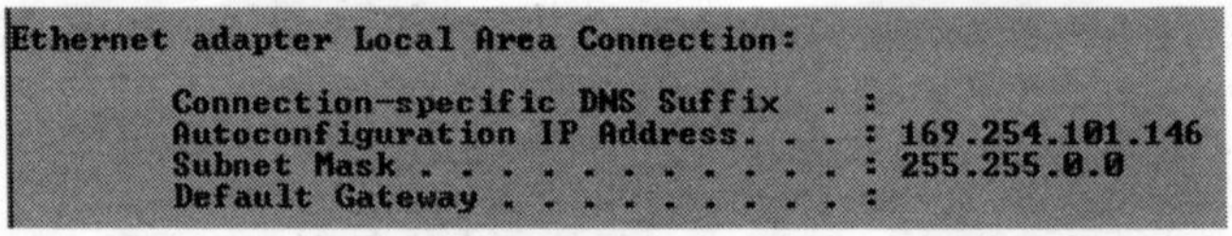

```
Ethernet adapter Local Area Connection:

        Connection-specific DNS Suffix  . :
        Autoconfiguration IP Address. . . : 169.254.101.146
        Subnet Mask . . . . . . . . . . . : 255.255.0.0
        Default Gateway . . . . . . . . . :
```

Figure 15.03

The address shown in the figure is in range reserved for Automatic Private IP Addressing (APIPA). This indicates that the workstation is failing to connect to a DHCP server. This could be a connectivity failure on the workstation – a node problem – or a fault with the DHCP server itself – a network problem that will affect all attached DHCP clients. This topic has been covered more fully in Chapter 6, *Expanding your network*.

Note: if you are using Linux or a Linux-based system the command IFCONFIG has much the same functionality (plus a bit) as IPCONFIG on Windows systems.

16.3 Troubleshooting the server

Your server box is just a PC like any other, albeit a more powerful one, perhaps. Certainly, in hardware terms, you need to check the obvious: hardware, power and connectivity before looking at anything more recondite. After you have ruled out the obvious then you will need to get down to the detail of your network operating system. All operating systems maintain logs which record various system events and messages. On Windows systems, the event viewer – type EVENTVWR at a system prompt to launch it – will show various logs and warning messages. Figure 15.04 shows this on an XP machine.

Figure 15.04

SME maintains similar logs. Access the server as admin using the server–manager tool and click on **View log files** from the **Administration** menu. This will give you access to a drop-down list of all the system logs. Figure 15.05 shows the last few lines of the boot log of the SME server Victoria.

```
Aug 25 16:42:13 victoria rc: Starting smb:  succeeded
Aug 25 16:42:42 victoria atalk: atalkd startup succeeded
Aug 25 16:42:54 victoria atalk: papd startup succeeded
Aug 25 16:42:54 victoria atalk: afpd startup succeeded
Aug 25 17:10:29 victoria dhcpd: Stopping dhcpd succeeded
Aug 25 17:11:55 victoria dhcpd: Stopping dhcpd succeeded
```

Figure 15.05

From these lines we can see that the SMB service started at boot time – just as well, because it is the SAMBA server that enables us to use our Windows network. The next three entries – the ones containing 'atalk' – are all concerned with aspects of providing support for the old Macintosh 'Appletalk' protocol. If there are no Mac machines on the network, running these services will do no harm, though it is of course wasteful of resources. The final two lines show that the DCHP service has been turned off – fine if that's what you wanted.

The trick with log files is not being overwhelmed with the amount of detail they provide. For most systems, there are online help forums and discussion groups, especially for open source products. These can usefully supplement your own knowledge and the documentation for your system.

16.4 Problems with modems and routers

Modem and router hardware is usually fairly robust. Most problems that aren't cured by a reboot are caused by wrong settings. Check the settings needed by your ISP, either through their website or through your documentation and re-enter them. In the case of a modem that needs drivers, reinstall and reconfigure with your ISP's settings. If necessary, replace your hardware.

16.5 Problems with printers

Most printing problems are caused by bad stock (paper that has been stored in damp conditions, for example), toner or ink running out, lack of mains power. Most printers have some form of diagnostic mode built into them, so before looking for network problems, test for a local solution.

1 Put some standard paper from a new ream in the paper tray.

2 Restart the printer.

3 Run the printer's built-in diagnostics and print a test page – you'll probably need to look at the manual for your particular printer to find out how to do this.

If this self-test produces a readable test page, then you probably have a connectivity or a software problem. To investigate this:

1 Check physical connections.

2 Reset the printer.

3 Reset the PC, server or access box to which it is attached. If you are using a printer attached to a Windows PC make sure that it is shared on the network.

4 From another PC on the network, navigate through the **Add Printer Wizard** using the Browse feature to list the printers on the system. If you can connect to the printer that you are troubleshooting, print a test page.

5 If you still can't print, reinstall.

In the case of a network device with its own IP address you can, of course, use the PING utility to see if it is visible. If it is not, check the IP address on the device, reset if necessary, and then try again.

Summary

In this chapter we have looked at some approaches to troubleshooting on a small LAN. The key word in troubleshooting is 'systematic' – there are only so many things that can be wrong and the key to finding the answer is the systematic narrowing down of the possibilities until only one remains. Start with the obvious and work your way though the possibilities. You progress by forming a theory, testing it and proving yourself wrong (usually several times) until eventually you prove yourself right. There is no such thing, really, as a wrong answer in troubleshooting, because each wrong answer takes you a step closer to the right one. You haven't failed until you give up.

teach **yourself**®

From Advanced Sudoku to Zulu, you'll find everything you need in the **teach yourself** range, in books, on CD and on DVD. Visit **www.teachyourself.co.uk** for more details.

Advanced Sudoku & Kakuro
Afrikaans
Alexander Technique
Algebra
Ancient Greek
Applied Psychology
Arabic
Aromatherapy
Art History
Astrology
Astronomy
AutoCAD 2004
AutoCAD 2007
Ayurveda
Baby Massage and Yoga
Baby Signing
Baby Sleep
Bach Flower Remedies
Backgammon
Ballroom Dancing
Basic Accounting
Basic Computer Skills
Basic Mathematics
Beauty
Beekeeping
Beginner's Arabic Script
Beginner's Chinese
Beginner's Chinese Script

Beginner's Dutch
Beginner's French
Beginner's German
Beginner's Greek
Beginner's Greek Script
Beginner's Hindi
Beginner's Italian
Beginner's Japanese
Beginner's Japanese Script
Beginner's Latin
Beginner's Portuguese
Beginner's Russian
Beginner's Russian Script
Beginner's Spanish
Beginner's Turkish
Beginner's Urdu Script
Bengali
Better Bridge
Better Chess
Better Driving
Better Handwriting
Biblical Hebrew
Biology
Birdwatching
Blogging
Body Language
Book Keeping
Brazilian Portuguese

Bridge
Buddhism
Bulgarian
Business Chinese
Business French
Business Japanese
Business Plans
Business Spanish
Business Studies
Buying a Home in France
Buying a Home in Italy
Buying a Home in Portugal
Buying a Home in Spain
C++
Calculus
Calligraphy
Cantonese
Car Buying and Maintenance
Card Games
Catalan
Chess
Chi Kung
Chinese Medicine
Chinese
Christianity
Classical Music
Coaching
Collecting
Computing for the Over 50s
Consulting
Copywriting
Correct English
Counselling
Creative Writing
Cricket
Croatian
Crystal Healing
CVs
Czech
Danish
Decluttering
Desktop Publishing
Detox
Digital Photography
Digital Video & PC Editing

Dog Training
Drawing
Dream Interpretation
Dutch
Dutch Conversation
Dutch Dictionary
Dutch Grammar
Eastern Philosophy
Electronics
English as a Foreign Language
English for International Business
English Grammar
English Grammar as a Foreign
    Language
English Vocabulary
Entrepreneurship
Estonian
Ethics
Excel 2003
Feng Shui
Film Making
Film Studies
Finance for Non-Financial
    Managers
Finnish
Fitness
Flash 8
Flash MX
Flexible Working
Flirting
Flower Arranging
Franchising
French
French Conversation
French Dictionary
French Grammar
French Phrasebook
French Starter Kit
French Verbs
French Vocabulary
Freud
Gaelic
Gardening
Genetics
Geology

German
German Conversation
German Grammar
German Phrasebook
German Verbs
German Vocabulary
Globalization
Go
Golf
Good Study Skills
Great Sex
Greek
Greek Conversation
Greek Phrasebook
Growing Your Business
Guitar
Gulf Arabic
Hand Reflexology
Hausa
Herbal Medicine
Hieroglyphics
Hindi
Hinduism
Home PC Maintenance and
   Networking
How to DJ
How to Run a Marathon
How to Win at Casino Games
How to Win at Horse Racing
How to Win at Online Gambling
How To Win At Poker
How to Write A Blockbuster
Human Anatomy & Physiology
Hungarian
Icelandic
Improve Your French
Improve Your German
Improve Your Italian
Improve Your Spanish
Improving your Employability
Indian Head Massage
Indonesian
Instant French
Instant German
Instant Greek

Instant Italian
Instant Japanese
Instant Portuguese
Instant Russian
Instant Spanish
Irish
Irish Conversation
Irish Grammar
Islam
Italian
Italian Conversation
Italian Grammar
Italian Phrasebook
Italian Starter Kit
Italian Verbs
Italian Vocabulary
Japanese
Japanese Conversation
Java
JavaScript
Jazz
Jewellery Making
Judaism
Jung
Keeping a Rabbit
Keeping Aquarium Fish
Keeping Pigs
Keeping Poultry
Knitting
Korean
Latin American Spanish
Latin
Latin Dictionary
Latin Grammar
Latvian
Letter Writing Skills
Life at 50: For Men
Life at 50: For Women
Life Coaching
Linguistics
LINUX
Lithuanian
Magic
Mahjong
Malay

Managing Stress
Managing Your Own Career
Mandarin Chinese Conversation
Marketing
Marx
Massage
Mathematics
Meditation
Modern China
Modern Hebrew
Modern Persian
Mosaics
Music Theory
Mussolini's Italy
Nazi Germany
Negotiating
Nepali
New Testament Greek
NLP
Norwegian
Norwegian Conversation
Old English
One-Day French
One-Day French – the DVD
One-Day German
One-Day Greek
One-Day Italian
One-Day Portuguese
One-Day Spanish
One-Day Spanish – the DVD
Origami
Owning a Cat
Owning A Horse
Panjabi
PC Networking for your Small
    Business
Personal Safety and Self
    Defence
Philosophy
Philosophy of Mind
Philosophy of Religion
Photography
Photoshop
PHP with MySQL
Physics

Piano
Pilates
Planning Your Wedding
Polish
Polish Conversation
Politics
Portuguese
Portuguese Conversation
Portuguese Grammar
Portuguese Phrasebook
Postmodernism
Pottery
PowerPoint 2003
PR
Project Management
Psychology
Quick Fix French Grammar
Quick Fix German Grammar
Quick Fix Italian Grammar
Quick Fix Spanish Grammar
Quick Fix: Access 2002
Quick Fix: Excel 2000
Quick Fix: Excel 2002
Quick Fix: HTML
Quick Fix: Windows XP
Quick Fix: Word
Quilting
Recruitment
Reflexology
Reiki
Relaxation
Retaining Staff
Romanian
Running Your Own Business
Russian
Russian Conversation
Russian Grammar
Sage Line 50
Sanskrit
Screenwriting
Serbian
Setting Up A Small Business
Shorthand Pitman 2000
Sikhism
Singing

Slovene
Small Business Accounting
Small Business Health Check
Songwriting
Spanish
Spanish Conversation
Spanish Dictionary
Spanish Grammar
Spanish Phrasebook
Spanish Starter Kit
Spanish Verbs
Spanish Vocabulary
Speaking On Special Occasions
Speed Reading
Stalin's Russia
Stand Up Comedy
Statistics
Stop Smoking
Sudoku
Swahili
Swahili Dictionary
Swedish
Swedish Conversation
Tagalog
Tai Chi
Tantric Sex
Tap Dancing
Teaching English as a Foreign
    Language
Teams & Team Working
Thai
The British Empire
The British Monarchy from Henry
    VIII
The Cold War
The First World War
The History of Ireland
The Internet
The Kama Sutra
The Middle East Since 1945
The Second World War
Theatre
Time Management
Tracing Your Family History
Training

Travel Writing
Trigonometry
Turkish
Turkish Conversation
Twentieth Century USA
Typing
Ukrainian
Understanding Tax for Small
    Businesses
Understanding Terrorism
Urdu
Vietnamese
Visual Basic
Volcanoes
Watercolour Painting
Weight Control through Diet &
    Exercise
Welsh
Welsh Dictionary
Welsh Grammar
Wills & Probate
Windows XP
Wine Tasting
Winning at Job Interviews
Word 2003
World Cultures: China
World Cultures: England
World Cultures: Germany
World Cultures: Italy
World Cultures: Japan
World Cultures: Portugal
World Cultures: Russia
World Cultures: Spain
World Cultures: Wales
World Faiths
Writing a Novel
Writing Crime Fiction
Writing for Children
Writing for Magazines
Writing Poetry
Xhosa
Yiddish
Yoga
Zen
Zulu